my revisi⊙n notes

AQA GCSE (9–1)

HISTORY
RUSSIA, 1894–1945: TSARDOM AND COMMUNISM

Matthew Fearns-Davies

HODDER
EDUCATION
AN HACHETTE UK COMPANY

Orders: please contact Hachette UK Distribution, Hely Hutchinson Centre, Milton Road, Didcot, Oxfordshire, OX11 7HH. Telephone: +44 (0)1235 827827. Email education@hachette.co.uk Lines are open from 9 a.m. to 5 p.m., Monday to Friday. You can also order through our website: www.hoddereducation.co.uk

ISBN: 9781398310186

© Matthew Fearns-Davies 2021

First published in 2021 by

Hodder Education,

An Hachette UK Company

Carmelite House
50 Victoria Embankment
London EC4Y 0DZ

www.hoddereducation.co.uk

Impression number 10 9 8 7 6 5 4

Year   2025 2024 2023

Cover photo © Aliaksandr – stock.adobe.com
Illustrations by Integra Software Services Ltd.
Typeset in India by Integra Software Services Ltd.
Printed in Great Britain by Ashford Colour Press Ltd

A catalogue record for this title is available from the British Library.

My revision planner

World History Period Study

How the Period Study will be examined

Overview of the Period Study – Russia, 1894–1945: Tsardom and communism

Period Studies are about understanding the narrative (story) across a period of important change or developments:

- Each study focuses on one country and its domestic history (rather than the international situation) over a 50-year period.

- Each focuses on two key related developments and the impact these developments had on people.

- You investigate these developments from different perspectives: political, social and cultural, economic, the role of ideas and of key individuals and groups.

- You will also need to understand and evaluate interpretations of the period you have studied.

There are a number of key skills you will need for the Period Study

Comprehending interpretations – you will need to be able to read an interpretation of this period and pick out features which reveal its viewpoint

Clearly describing – you will need to be able to give a short but detailed description of a key event or development

THE PERIOD STUDY

Evaluating interpretations – you will need to be able to look carefully at the content and provenance of two interpretations and explain why they have different viewpoints. You will also need to compare these to your own knowledge to give a judgement about their accuracy

Explaining – you will need to identify but also explain the impact of a development

Coming to overall judgements and supporting them – you will need to make sophisticated judgements based upon the range of evidence used in your answer. You will need to write these in a clear and persuasive manner

There are four main question types in the British Depth Study exam

This is Section A of Paper 1. It is worth 40 marks in total. You will be asked the following types of question.

1 How do interpretations differ? *(4 marks)*

You will be given two interpretations and will need to work out what each is arguing. You will then need to consider how similar or different these arguments are. The focus in question 1 is on the content of the interpretations.

2 Why do interpretations differ? *(4 marks)*

You will have to explain why the interpretations you have looked at are different. This will involve looking at the provenance of the interpretations and then explaining reasons why they might have different views.

3 How convincing are these interpretations? *(8 marks)*

You will use your own contextual knowledge of the period to evaluate how accurate (convincing) the content of the interpretations is. You will need to support and challenge the claims made in both interpretations.

Questions 1–3 are closely linked. They deal with the same two interpretations.

The rest of the questions test your knowledge and understanding and are not based on the interpretations.

4 Describe ... *(4 marks)*

You will need to give a brief but precise summary of a key topic, event or development using specific factual knowledge.

5 In what ways ... ? *(8 marks)*

You will be asked to explain how a key development affected a situation or a group of people. You will need to use specific factual knowledge to show the impacts of this development.

6 Essay question *(12 marks)*

You will be given two factors, events or individuals and asked to evaluate the extent of their importance or impact, or how extensive the impact of a key development was on them. You will need to structure your answer as an essay, include a range of factual detail and come to a judgement.

How we help you develop your exam skills

- The revision tasks help you build understanding and skills step by step. For example:

  Eliminate irrelevance will help you to focus on the question.

  Develop the explanation will help you to make your writing more analytical.

  Spot the interpretation will help you to identify arguments in an interpretation.

  Support or challenge will help you to write balanced essays.

- The practice questions give you exam-style questions.
- Exam focus on pages 44–47 gives you model answers for each question type.

Plus:
There are **annotated model answers** for every practice question online at www. hoddereducation.co.uk/myrevisionnotes downloads.

1.1 Russia's economy and society

> **Key point**
>
> Industrialisation from the late nineteenth century had economic, social and political consequences which became very important in 1917. Production increased, which pleased the Tsar. However, as more people moved to cities looking for work and experienced the terrible living and working conditions, the demands for reform and support for opposition groups increased.

Russia was becoming industrialised and production was increasing towards the end of the nineteenth century

- Tsars Alexander II and Alexander III had wanted Russia to become an industrial power to compete with other European countries.
- Sergei Witte was Nicholas II's Finance Minister and his policies aimed to expand Russia's industrialisation programme.
- Oil, coal and iron production almost trebled between 1890 and 1900 in a period labelled by some historians as the 'Great Spurt' to indicate the rapid progress in industrialisation.
- The small middle class of lawyers, doctors and shopkeepers became much larger as they were joined by **capitalists** – industrialists, bankers, traders and businessmen.

Workers in the cities experienced terrible living and working conditions

- The populations of cities such as Moscow and St Petersburg grew rapidly as peasants moved there for work. Some returned to the countryside for the harvest.
- Some of the problems experienced by workers included overcrowded living conditions, poor food quality, disease and alcoholism.
- Workers could not challenge the brutal discipline or twelve-to-fifteen-hour days as trade unions were illegal.
- The government did nothing to stop child labour or ensure workers' safety.
- The capitalists were interested in making profit and controlling their workers and this often led to clashes which would become more and more important up to 1917.

Peasants in the countryside experienced terrible living and working conditions

- Eighty per cent of the Russian population were peasants. Famines occurred regularly in the countryside and life expectancy was only 40 years of age.
- Land was in short supply as the population had increased by 50 per cent between 1860 and 1897 and much of the land in Russia was unsuitable for farming. There was a small group of rich peasants called kulaks.
- The **mir** divided land up among a village community with each family receiving a strip and using ancient farming methods. For most peasants the living and working conditions were terrible.
- Religion (the Russian Orthodox Church) was very important to peasants and most supported the Tsar because their local priest told them to be loyal.
- Some peasants began to support opposition groups such as the **Socialist Revolutionaries** due to anger about how much land the **aristocracy**, church and Tsar owned.

The aristocracy was mostly wealthy and powerful

- The aristocracy represented only about 1.5 per cent of the population but owned about 25 per cent of the land. It was an important group in supporting the Tsar and the autocratic system.
- Aristocrats were often very wealthy and had very comfortable lives either in the countryside or in the cities. Those in the countryside controlled the peasants on their estates. Some of those in the cities began to make money by investing in new industries.
- Landowners often had roles in the **zemstva** or even in the Tsar's government. They were loyal to the Tsar and did not want Russia to change.
- A few aristocrats were struggling financially and had to sell their land.
- There was fear about peasant uprisings and land seizures by those who worked on the land.

Test yourself

1 Who were the capitalists and what were they interested in achieving?
2 Why were most peasants loyal to the Tsar?

 Topic summary

Complete the following mind map to summarise the state of the Russian economy and society at the end of the nineteenth century.

This will make it easier to write analytical answers. Try to be as specific as possible as the mark schemes ask you to use specific, detailed knowledge. The first one has been started for you.

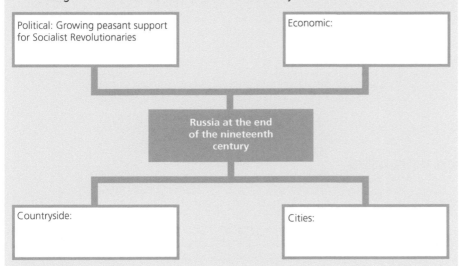

 Practice question

Describe two problems faced by the Tsarist regime at the end of the nineteenth century. **(4 marks)**

 Structure the detail

Question 5 of your exam focuses on how a key development affected a situation or a group of people. For example:

In what ways were the lives of Russians affected by industrialisation at the end of the nineteenth century? **(8 marks)**

Here are some facts about industrialisation at the end of the nineteenth century. Turn these into a paragraph that could form part of your answer to the question.

A Alcoholism was common.
B The population of Russia doubled between 1860 and 1897.
C Disease spread quickly.
D Working days in a factory were between twelve and fifteen hours on average.
E Trade unions were illegal.
F Many peasants moved to cities such as St Petersburg and Moscow.

TIP

You should be writing two paragraphs in answer to an 8-mark question. Make sure you consider a different impact or change in each paragraph. If your first paragraph considers difficulties in the cities, your second paragraph could explore new opportunities for the aristocracy. Considering the impact on different groups will allow you to make a short comparison of impact and access the top level of the mark scheme.

1.2 Nicholas II's autocracy and the growth of revolutionary opposition

Nicholas II was an ineffective Tsar controlling an autocratic system

Autocratic system	Nicholas' individual style
• The Tsarist regime had not granted any political rights to the Russian people • The Tsar could appoint whoever he wanted to government positions • Local governors and zemstva helped to control Russia • The mir controlled peasants but could be overruled by land captains (usually minor landlords) • Emergency laws allowed the police to arrest suspected opponents of Tsarism, censor newspapers and issue fines • 10,000 police officers dealt with political opponents • The Okhrana spied on suspected opponents of the regime • The army and Cossacks dealt with rebellions	• Committed to autocracy and believed that God had chosen him to rule • Appointed friends and family to government positions regardless of their ability • Nicholas was a poor manager, refusing to chair the Council of Ministers and meeting ministers individually. This created rivalry between government departments • Talented Chief Ministers were sacked – Sergei Witte in 1906 and Peter Stolypin was assassinated before Nicholas could sack him in 1911 • Wasted time with small tasks such as appointing provincial midwives rather than delegating and dealing with nationwide matters

Revolutionary opposition increased at the start of the twentieth century

There were three main opposition groups at the beginning of the twentieth century.

Group	Aims	Supporters	Actions
Socialist Revolutionaries	Wanted to divide nobles' land among the peasantry	Support from some in the towns and larger numbers of peasants	Assassinated politicians and members of the Okhrana
Social Democratic Party	Wanted a revolution to overthrow the Tsar. Many members were arrested, exiled to Siberia or fled abroad	Supported by workers and some soldiers	Created in 1898, the group split into two in 1903 – the Bolsheviks led by Lenin who wanted revolution immediately and the Mensheviks who wanted to wait
Cadets	Wanted a greater level of democracy but to keep the Tsar	Mostly middle class	Political party established in late 1905. They argued for the creation of a Duma and then for further reforms when the Duma met

The October Manifesto helped to end the 1905 revolution

- January 1905, Bloody Sunday: Father Gapon led 200,000 peaceful protesters to the Winter Palace in St Petersburg with a petition asking for changes. Tsarist troops opened fire, killing over 100 and injuring hundreds more.

- Protests and strikes continued throughout 1905. Over 2.8 million workers participated in 14,000 strikes. There were many peasant rebellions in the countryside.

- Soviets were established in around 80 towns around Russia in 1905. The most important were in St Petersburg and Moscow. They were a sign that many Russian people wanted to be involved in governing the country.

- In June 1905 sailors on the Battleship *Potemkin* mutinied in support of striking workers.

- The October Manifesto saved Tsarism. In it, the Tsar promised to create a Duma (elected assembly) and grant freedom of speech and the right to form political parties.

- The Manifesto divided the Tsar's opponents. The army was used to crush remaining opposition including the soviets.

Key point

Nicholas ruled as Russia faced economic and social change and opposition to an unpopular system. He was unwilling and unable to adapt to these changes in order to retain the support of the Russian people.

Support or challenge

In your exams you will often have to reach a judgement and support it with evidence. This task helps you practise. Read this statement:

'By the end of 1905 the Tsarist system was very strong.'

Below is evidence from this period. For each piece of evidence, decide whether it supports or challenges the overall statement above.

Statement	Support	Challenge
The Tsar had a specially trained part of the military called Cossacks to deal with rebellion		
Nicholas II was not good at delegating and dealt with a lot of small issues personally		
Landowners who were traditionally loyal to the Tsar were often local governors		
Peasants and workers were not very well represented in zemstva		
There were many strikes and peasant uprisings during 1905 including Bloody Sunday		
The October Manifesto promised to increase people's rights including the creation of a Duma (elected assembly)		
Emergency laws allowed the Tsar to censor books and newspapers		
There had been an increase in support for opposition groups such as the Socialist Revolutionaries		

Spot the interpretation

Look at Interpretation A. Next to it are some inferences that you can draw from it.

1 Link each inference to specific details in the interpretation.
2 For each inference, add a specific piece of your own knowledge that supports or challenges this inference.

INTERPRETATION A *Sergei Witte*

I pity the Tsar. I pity Russia. He is a poor and unhappy sovereign. What did he inherit and what will he leave? He is obviously a good and quite intelligent man, but he lacks willpower, and it is from that character that his state defects developed, that is, his defects as a ruler, especially an autocratic and absolute ruler.

A Nicholas did not enjoy being Tsar.
B Nicholas did have some abilities.
C Nicholas was not forceful or determined enough.
D Nicholas was not equipped to be the leader of an autocratic state.

Test yourself

1 List three opposition groups at the beginning of the twentieth century.
2 List three examples of protest during the 1905 revolution.

TIP

To access Level 4 of the mark scheme when answering an 8-mark change question try to explain how the event or situation affected different groups of people in different ways. At the end of your answer make a direct comparison between the two groups you have considered.

Practice question

In what ways were the lives of the Russian people affected by the 1905 revolution?   (8 marks)

1.3 Reforms in Russia, 1905–14

Dumas were less critical of the Tsar after electoral laws were changed

- The Duma met for the first time in 1906. Its power was severely limited as the Tsar had created a **State Council** and a **Council of Ministers**. The State Council was half elected by the zemstva and half appointed by the Tsar, it was very conservative and opposed making changes to the country.

- The First and Second Dumas lasted for less than a year before being dismissed by the Tsar. The deputies in these Dumas were mostly members of **radical** or **reformist** parties such as the Cadets and the **Trudoviks**. They were disappointed as they did not have any real power.

- The electoral laws were changed in 1907 before the Third Duma which meant there were far fewer deputies elected who would criticise or oppose the Tsar's policies. Most deputies were now members of rightist parties such as the **Octobrists**.

- The Third Duma completed its full five-year term. Even this 'loyal' Duma had begun to criticise the Tsar by 1912. The Tsar continued to rule as if the Duma did not exist.

> **Key point**
>
> The 1905 revolution had demonstrated a desire for change among the Russian population. Nicholas ignored that desire because he firmly believed he had been chosen by God to rule autocratically. He didn't appear in public after 1905 until 1913. The result was that the Tsar did not understand the Russian people and the people lost respect for him.

Stolypin used harsh repression to control the countryside and introduced economic reforms with mixed results

- Peter Stolypin (Chief Minister 1906–11) famously said, 'First pacification, then reform.' He wanted to wipe out opposition to the Tsar and then transform the economy, especially in relation to agriculture.

Oppression	Reform
• Twenty thousand protesters were exiled to places such as Siberia • Over 1,000 protesters and revolutionaries were hanged (the noose used to hang people was nicknamed 'Stolypin's necktie')	• Wealthier peasants – kulaks – were allowed to opt out of the village commune and buy land • A Peasants' Land Bank was created to loan kulaks money to help them buy land and invest in it • Stolypin tried to boost Russian industry by continuing to invest in the building of railways

Stolypin's reforms had some successes

- 1890–1913: grain production doubled.
- 1890–1913: pig iron production increased and coal production more than tripled.
- The number of strikes halved between 1908 and 1911 and peasant disturbances were under control until after 1914.

Stolypin's reforms had some failures

- Ninety per cent of land in the west of Russia remained under the control of the mir in 1916.
- Wages remained low and the cost of food and housing remained high.
- Even in the Russian empire's best farmland in Ukraine the farms remained small.

After Stolypin's death public support for the Tsar decreased

- Nicholas did not want change and prevented Stolypin from introducing basic education and regulations to protect factory workers.
- Nicholas was about to replace Stolypin when he was assassinated in 1911.
- Oppression continued when soldiers opened fire on striking workers at the Lena Goldfields in 1912; 250 were killed and people were reminded of Bloody Sunday.
- 1913 saw an excellent harvest and celebrations of the 300th anniversary of Romanov rule but an economic downturn in 1912 meant many Russians were frustrated by unemployment and hunger as well as oppression.

Test yourself

1 List two successes and two failures for Stolypin.

2 Why wasn't Nicholas very popular by 1913?

Develop the detail

Each of the statements below is vague and lacks detail. On a separate piece of paper, add details to show that you understand the general point made. One example has been done for you.

Generalised statement	With developed detail
The Duma did not have much power	A State Council had been created which prevented the Duma from passing laws to decrease the power of the Tsar
Stolypin used oppression to reduce opposition	
Agriculture was reformed from 1906	
Industry continued to develop after 1905	

Eliminate irrelevance

Describe **two** ways in which Russia changed after 1905. (4 marks)

The answer below contains material which is not necessary for a question like this. Cross out any material which you think might be irrelevant to the question.

Stolypin was the Chief Minister from 1906 to 1911, replacing Sergei Witte who had been Chief Minister in 1905 and Finance Minister before that. Stolypin introduced reforms to agriculture which allowed more successful peasants to leave the village commune and buy their own land. This was a change because previously the village elders had controlled the land. Other European countries had begun to introduce democratic reforms in the nineteenth century. In 1906 the Duma met for the first time. This was an elected assembly which had never been allowed in Russia before and gave some political parties the chance to legally share their views and even criticise the Tsar. The Tsar did not like being criticised and was opposed to change, he tried and failed to prevent Russia from changing.

Practice question

Which of the following was the more important reason in helping the Tsar maintain control between 1906 and 1913?

- Reform
- Oppression

Explain your answer with reference to both reasons. (12 marks)

TIP

Make sure you are using the key words from the question to focus your answer and ensure you are explaining your examples. In response to this question you should be explaining how each example was 'helping the Tsar maintain control'.

1.4 The impact of the First World War

The outbreak of the First World War resulted in a brief improvement in the Tsar's popularity

- In August 1914 Russia entered the First World War.
- Peasants, workers and aristocrats were caught up in displays of patriotism.
- There was praise for the Tsar's actions.
- Anti-government strikes and demonstrations were abandoned.
- The positive feeling did not last long because the war did not bring the victories that the Russian people expected.

Military defeats and poor organisation increased support for revolutionary parties

- Initially soldiers were enthusiastic about fighting for their country.
- Russian soldiers fought bravely but suffered major defeats at Tannenburg and the Masurian Lakes.
- The largely aristocratic officers were mostly ineffective military leaders and treated the soldiers badly.
- There were shortages of rifles, ammunition, artillery and shells and many soldiers did not even have boots.
- In September 1915 the Tsar took personal command of the army. He was not an able commander and was personally blamed for the continuing military defeats.
- By 1917 many soldiers were angry and had started to support the revolutionary Bolshevik Party.

> **Key point**
>
> The First World War placed huge pressure upon the Tsarist system. Poor organisation and leadership, which was based on position in society rather than ability, resulted in military defeat and anger from the population towards the Tsar and Tsarism.

The war had devastating social and economic consequences

Social effects	Economic effects

Countryside
• The army was largely made up of peasants and casualty figures were huge – 9.15 million for the entire war
• Workload increased for women and children as so many peasants were conscripted but production fell
• 13% of the village of Grushkeva was killed, leaving many widows and orphans
• War pensions were not always paid to widows of fallen soldiers
 	
Cities
• Overcrowded living conditions were even worse than before the war
• Although there were resources available there were often shortages of food and fuel because the railway network could not cope with the needs of the army, industry and city-dwellers
• Long bread queues increased resentment towards the Tsar
	Countryside
	• Peasants who had extra grain were able to make money supplying the government. However, only small prices were paid for these goods
	• There was limited availability of household goods and tools
	
	Cities
	• War contracts created an extra 3.5 million industrial jobs but workers did not receive higher wages
	• The average worker's wage in 1917 was five roubles a day and prices had increased throughout the war:
	  ▪ A worker could buy a third of a bag of flour with their wage in 1917 in comparison with two bags of flour in 1914
	  ▪ A worker could buy three-quarters of a bag of potatoes in 1917 in comparison with five bags in 1914
	  ▪ A worker could buy 0.8 kilograms of meat in 1917 in comparison with 5 kilograms in 1914

Topic summary

Copy and complete this topic summary pyramid to summarise the key details of the topic.

- **One** date that the Tsar took control of the army
- **Two** battles in which the Russian army was defeated
- **Three** groups in society caught up in displays of patriotism
- **Four** social impacts of the First World War
- **Five** shortages experienced by the Russian army
- **Six** economic impacts of the First World War

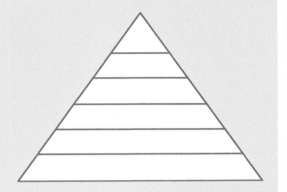

Develop the explanation

Complete the table to explain why each of these examples had an impact on the lives of the Russian people. The first one has been completed for you.

Examples	Explanations of impact upon the Russian people
The Russian army suffered 9.15 million casualties in the First World War	This had a significant impact on people's morale as well as their quality of life. Family members were devastated by the loss of or injury to their loved ones. Widows would often fail to receive war pensions and struggled without their husbands' wages
The average worker's wage would buy only three-quarters of a bag of potatoes in 1917	
The railway network could not cope with the demands of the army, industry and the populations of the cities	
Peasants with extra grain were able to sell this to the government for low prices	

Test yourself

1 Why did the Tsar's popularity briefly improve at the beginning of the war?
2 List two methods of opposition which stopped at the start of the war.
3 Why was the Tsar personally blamed for military defeats?

Practice question

Describe two problems faced by the Tsar during the First World War. (4 marks)

> **TIP**
>
> To make sure you get your timing right in the exam try to spend five minutes for every 4 marks available. A 4-mark describe question should only take a total of five minutes to answer.

1.5 The unpopularity of the Romanovs

Key point

Before the war there were many people in Russia who supported Tsarism, but by 1917 a number of organisations had been established that offered alternatives to Tsarist rule. The Russian people were so frustrated with Nicholas' poor decisions that many were willing to try a new form of government.

The war and poor choices made the Romanovs unpopular with the aristocracy

- Junior officers who were the next generation of the aristocratic class suffered high casualties during the war.
- Aristocrats' incomes were threatened as 13 million peasants who would usually work on landowners' estates had been conscripted into the army.
- An organisation called Zemgor brought together regional and town councils and began to organise the distribution of medical supplies and uniforms. Zemgor was performing the Tsarist government's job.
- Some Cadet, Octobrist and other deputies in the Duma created the Progressive Bloc which called for the Tsar to share power with them in order to help with the war effort. Nicholas' refusal convinced some deputies that the Tsarist system was not working.
- The aristocracy was appalled by Nicholas' decision to take command of the army and leave his German wife and Rasputin in charge in Petrograd (which had been renamed from St Petersburg to sound less German).
- By 1916 even the Council of the United Nobility wanted Nicholas to step down.

Nicholas unwisely allowed Rasputin to have great influence which alienated the aristocracy

- The Romanovs allowed an unusual character called Rasputin to have influence in the family and eventually government. The Romanovs believed he could help their son, Alexei, who was ill with a blood disease called haemophilia.
- Many Russians disapproved of Rasputin's lifestyle of drinking and womanising and were dismayed that the Romanovs listened to him. The Tsar and his family were supposed to represent the values of the Russian Orthodox Church.
- Rasputin seemed to have particular influence over the Tsarina Alexandra. There were even rumours of an affair between them. Alexandra took his chaotic advice about government ministers. Four different

departments all changed ministers three times in the year after the Tsar moved to army headquarters. Cartoons in newspapers showed Alexandra as a German spy working with Rasputin to undermine the war effort.

- The Tsar's opponents claimed Rasputin's influence proved Nicholas was incapable of ruling Russia. Even Mikhail Rodzianko, the President of the Fourth Duma, personally warned the Tsar about the damage Rasputin was doing to his reputation.
- Opposition to Rasputin was so serious that he was murdered by a group of aristocrats in December 1916.

Rebel soldiers and mass protests resulted in the Tsar's abdication

- From August 1914 to 1917 the number of strikes by factory workers increased from 50 to 1,300.
- In January 1917 strikes again broke out in some cities. By February 1917 strikes were joined by some of the newer, less experienced soldiers.
- 8 March: International Women's Day saw thousands of female marchers in Petrograd joined by workers protesting for bread and striking workers from the Putilov Steel factory.
- 7–10 March: 250,000 workers were on strike and industry was at a standstill. More soldiers joined the strikes so workers became bolder and more political in their protests. They began to call for an end to the war and to Tsarism.
- 12 March:
  - Members of the Duma created a Provisional Committee to take over the government from the Tsar.
  - The Tsar ordered soldiers to put down the revolt by force but the soldiers refused. Some officers were shot by their own soldiers.
  - The Petrograd Soviet was established by revolutionaries and took control of food supplies. The authority of army officers was undermined as the Soviet helped to set up soldiers' committees.
- 15 March: the Tsar abdicated. Nicholas tried to pass the throne to his brother Michael. He refused, which brought an end to over 300 years of Romanov rule.

✎ Test yourself

1 List three reasons for the Tsar's unpopularity with the aristocracy.
2 Who was Rasputin and what happened to him in the end?
3 What does abdication mean?

Topic summary

Complete the following mind map to summarise the reasons that resulted in the Tsar's abdication. Use the information over the last seven pages and your own knowledge.

This will make it easier to write analytical answers. Try to be as specific as possible as the mark schemes ask you to use specific, detailed knowledge. The first one has been started for you.

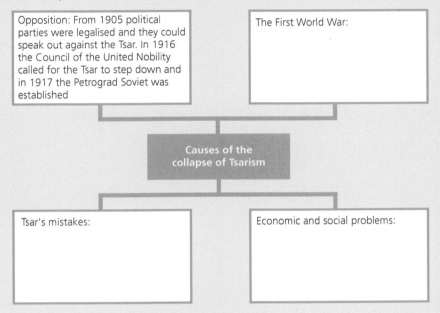

Opposition: From 1905 political parties were legalised and they could speak out against the Tsar. In 1916 the Council of the United Nobility called for the Tsar to step down and in 1917 the Petrograd Soviet was established

The First World War:

Causes of the collapse of Tsarism

Tsar's mistakes:

Economic and social problems:

 Practice questions

Read Interpretations A and B and then answer the questions that follow.

INTERPRETATION A *Leon Trotsky from his book,* The History of the Russian Revolution, *1932.*

Nicholas II inherited from his ancestors not only a giant empire, but also a revolution. And they did not bequeath [pass on to] him one quality which would have made him capable of governing an empire or even a province or a county.

INTERPRETATION B *An extract from* Always with Honour, *the memoirs of General Peter Wrangel, published in 1957. Wrangel was a general in the Russian army and then served in the White Army during the Civil War.*

Those of us who loved our country and the Army were terribly anxious at the continual changes in the Ministry, the conflicts between the government and the Duma, the ever-increasing number of petitions and appeals addressed to the Tsar by many influential organisations, each one demanding popular control, and above all, by the alarming rumours concerning certain persons in the Tsar's entourage.

1 How does Interpretation B differ from Interpretation A about the unpopularity of the Tsar? Explain your answer based on what it says in Interpretations A and B.   (4 marks)

2 Why might the authors of Interpretations A and B have a different interpretation about the unpopularity of the Tsar?   (4 marks)

3 Which interpretation gives the more convincing opinion about the unpopularity of the Tsar? Explain your answer based on your contextual knowledge and what it says in Interpretations A and B.   (8 marks)

TIP

When answering Question 2 about interpretations look carefully at all the information about who has written the extracts. Use what you know about the different backgrounds of the authors to help explain why they would have different views about the topic in the question.

2.1 The failures of the Provisional Government

The Provisional Government faced a range of **social, economic and military problems**

Problems for the Provisional Government	Actions taken by the Provisional Government
• whether to continue fighting in the war • whether to approve peasant seizures of land that were already happening or ask peasants to wait • how to get food to the cities where many were starving	• not always agreement about how to respond to problems. Members included politicians from the pro-reform Cadets and the conservative Octobrists. • Russia promised Britain and France to continue with the war effort • peasants were asked to wait for elections before seizing land. Food prices doubled between February and June as problems with the railway, a poor harvest and peasant reluctance to bring grain to the cities meant food shortages continued

> **Key point**
>
> The Tsar's abdication created a power vacuum which was filled by the Dual Authority.
> The two parts to this 'dual' authority were:
> 1 Provisional Government – largely members of the Duma's Provisional Committee
> 2 Petrograd Soviet – a council of soldiers, workers and peasant deputies.
>
> The two organisations met in the same building, the Tauride Palace, but struggled to work together.

- The Provisional Government had the responsibility for passing laws but was not designed to last forever. Elections were be held for a Constituent Assembly which would be democratic and represent Russian people's views.
- The Petrograd Soviet became increasingly powerful. It was supported by industrial workers and communications workers as well as the military.
- Soviet Order Number 1 committed soldiers to following orders from the Provisional Government only if the Soviet agreed.
- One person, Alexander Kerensky, was a member of the Provisional Government (Justice Minister) and the Soviet.

The **Provisional Government's authority collapsed during the second half of 1917**

September, Kornilov Affair: The army was disintegrating and crime was increasing. Kerensky appointed Lavr Kornilov as Supreme Commander of the Russian forces in an attempt to restore order. Kornilov started moving troops towards the capital to restore order but some thought he was trying to seize control. Kerensky panicked and issued weapons to the Soviet's Red Guards. The Bolsheviks played a key role in organising the defence of the capital. They persuaded railway workers to redirect trains carrying Kornilov's troops and some soldiers to desert Kornilov.

July Offensive: In the face of defeats and desertions Kerensky organised a huge offensive. It was a disaster. There were tens of thousands of casualties and more territory was lost to Germany. Desertions increased as peasants left the army to join in with the land seizures.

October/November Revolution: The Bolsheviks seized power and the Provisional Government collapsed

July Days: Some Bolsheviks with soldiers, sailors and workers marched to the Tauride Palace to demand that the Soviet take power for itself. The Soviet leaders, who were not Bolsheviks, refused. The Provisional Government released a letter showing that the German government had helped Lenin get into Russia. Troops who wanted to continue working with the Provisional Government restored order. The Bolsheviks were in disarray and Lenin fled to Finland.

End of September: Bolshevik popularity soared as Kerensky's plummeted. Kerensky lost soldiers' and workers' support due to military defeats and food shortages and he stopped the peasants seizing land. Bolshevik majorities were elected to the soviets of most major towns and cities including Petrograd and Moscow.

Timeline of the Provisional Government

Test yourself

1 List three urgent problems for the Provisional Government in 1917.
2 What was the Kornilov Affair and why did it make the Bolsheviks look good?

 Develop the detail

Each of the statements below is vague and lacks detail. On a separate piece of paper, add further details to show that you understand the general point made. One example has been done for you.

Generalised statement	With developed detail
The members of the Provisional Government did not automatically agree	There were many different views and backgrounds in the Provisional Government, from former members of the Duma who supported change, such as the Cadets, to those who wanted to limit popular involvement in government, such as the Octobrists
The Petrograd Soviet limited the power of the Provisional Government	
Peasants were disappointed with the Provisional Government	
The Provisional Government was unable to change Russia's military fortunes during the First World War	

 Essay plan

Which of the following was the more important reason for the Provisional Government's loss of popularity by the end of September 1917?

- **Continuing Russian involvement in the First World War**
- **The Kornilov Affair**

Explain your answer with reference to both bullet points. **(12 marks)**

Plan this essay:
1 Write a list of points you would use to support each bullet point.
2 Decide which bullet point you think was more important. Then write your essay conclusion.

TIP

To access the top level of the mark scheme in essay questions use the conclusion to make a link between the two bullet points. The link should show how the issue in one bullet point was more important in answering the question by causing or developing the issue in the other bullet point.

 Practice question

Describe two problems faced by the Provisional Government. (4 marks)

2.2 The growth of Bolshevik organisation and the October/November Revolution

Key point

The Bolsheviks did not play an important role in the Tsar's abdication but decisive action saw them seize power at the end of 1917. Soldiers and sailors, impressed by the Bolsheviks' opposition to the war, provided the military forces behind the revolution.

Lenin played a key role in the growth of the Bolshevik Party

- Bolshevik leader Lenin had been involved in the 1905 revolution and was in exile in Europe until he returned to Russia after the Tsar's abdication. Germany provided a train to help Lenin return, hoping he would cause chaos in Russia.

- Lenin used propaganda such as his pamphlet the 'April Theses' which called for an introduction of Soviet government and a fairer wage system. Lenin's popular slogans included 'all power to the Soviets' and 'peace, bread and land'.

- Support for the Bolsheviks increased, especially among soldiers and in the soviets.

Lenin persuaded and Trotsky organised the Bolsheviks to carry out the October/November Revolution

- By the end of October, Lenin persuaded his Party that they could seize power despite leading Bolsheviks Zinoviev and Kamenev feeling that Russia was not ready.

- Leon Trotsky was a revolutionary who had been exiled under the Tsar. He published the revolutionary newspaper *Pravda*. He joined the Bolsheviks in September/October 1917 when he became Chairman of the Petrograd Soviet after the Bolsheviks won a majority.

- Trotsky organised the Red Guards in Petrograd. Some historians claim he was more important than Lenin in the October Revolution.

- During the night of 6 November the Red Guards took control of the post offices, bridges and state bank.

- On 7 November the Bolsheviks took control of railway stations and other targets and faced very little opposition. They stormed the Winter Palace without fighting and arrested the Ministers of the Provisional Government.

- Kerensky escaped from the capital and tried to save his position with the support of loyal troops. This failed and he fled into exile.

- On 8 November the Petrograd Soviet announced the Provisional Government had been overthrown and people could look forward to the end of war and an increase in their rights and freedoms.

The Bolsheviks seized power even without the support of the majority of the Russian people

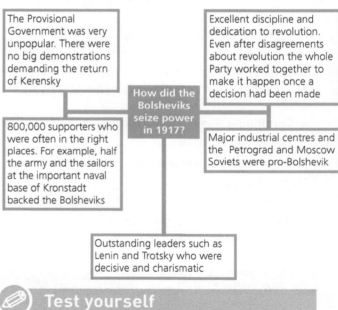

Test yourself

1 List three reasons that the Bolsheviks were able to seize power.

2 What role did Trotsky play in the October Revolution?

TIP

Don't let the dates of the events in 1917 confuse you. Russia used a calendar that was thirteen days behind the rest of Western Europe until it was changed in 1918. This means that the events of the 7–8 November were taking place 25–26 October according to the Russian calendar. This explains why you may see different terms used for the same events such as the 'June/July Offensive' and the 'October/November Revolution'.

Key events

Complete the flow chart below to show the key events in the October Revolution. The first box has been done for you.

Lenin convinced the Bolshevik Party that they should attempt to seize power → ☐ → ☐ → ☐ → ☐

 Develop the explanation

Complete the table to explain why each of these reasons led to the October Revolution. The first one has been done for you.

Reasons	Explanations
Unpopularity of the Provisional Government	The failures of the Provisional Government managed to turn groups of people from across Russian society against them. The military were unhappy about defeats during the First World War and the peasantry were angry about high casualty rates and attempts to stop them seizing land. The workers in cities were unhappy about food shortages and the Kornilov Affair made the Provisional Government look weak
Discipline of the Bolsheviks	
Bolshevik control of the cities	
Leadership	

 Practice Question

INTERPRETATION A *Alexander Kerensky*, The Catastrophe, *1927*.

The hours of the night dragged on painfully. From everywhere we expected reinforcements, but none appeared. There were endless telephone negotiations with the Cossack* regiments. Under various excuses the Cossacks stubbornly stuck to their barracks, asserting all the time that 'everything would be cleared up' within fifteen or twenty minutes and that they would then 'begin to saddle their horses' … Meanwhile the night hours passed … Not a word from the Cossacks.

*Cossacks were a special part of the army. The Tsarist regime had used Cossacks to crush opposition.

INTERPRETATION B *Leon Trotsky*, A History of the Russian Revolution, *1932*.

It was the most popular mass insurrection in all history … those invisible masses were marching more than ever before in step with the events … The Red Guard detachments felt at their back the support of the factories … Companies of the Red Guard had emerged from their districts. The worker with a rifle, the bayonet above hat or cap, the rifle-belt over a civilian coat – that is the essential image of the 25th of October. Cautiously … the armed worker was bringing order into the capital conquered by him.

1 How does Interpretation A differ from Interpretation B about the events of the October Revolution? Explain your answer based on what it says in Interpretations A and B. (4 marks)

2 Why might the authors of Interpretations A and B have a different interpretation about the events of the October Revolution? (4 marks)

3 Which interpretation gives the more convincing opinion about the events of the October Revolution? Explain your answer based on your contextual knowledge and what it says in Interpretations A and B. (8 marks)

2.3 Lenin's dictatorship and the end of the First World War

Lenin used decrees to win support and to begin to transform Russia

- Lenin and the Bolsheviks wanted to make Russia a **communist** country. Some supported communism but many landowners and factory owners knew it threatened their wealth.
- Lenin established a Council of People's Commissars (the **Sovnarkom**). It issued huge numbers of **decrees** designed to increase the Bolsheviks' power and popularity.

The decrees	How it helped the Bolsheviks
Land belonging to the Tsar, Church and nobles handed over to the peasants	Popular with peasants
Russia asked for peace with Germany	Popular with many Russians, especially the army and the peasantry
Maximum eight-hour working day	Popular with factory workers
Non-Bolshevik newspapers banned	Made criticising the Bolsheviks harder
Cadet Party banned	Reduced opportunities for opposition
Cheka (secret police) established (see page 22)	Dealt with opposition
Workers given control of factories	Popular with factory workers
Marriage without priests was allowed and divorce made easier	Popular with young people and those who wanted a more liberal country

> **Key point**
>
> The Bolsheviks had learned from the mistakes of the Tsarist regime and the Provisional Government. In order to retain power they would have to end Russian participation in the First World War, introduce popular reforms and deal ruthlessly with opposition. Lenin had to deliver on the promises of peace, bread and land.

The Constituent Assembly was closed to prevent opposition to the Bolsheviks developing

- Free elections to the **Constituent Assembly** were held in late 1917. The Bolsheviks did not win a majority. The results are shown in the table on the right.
- Lenin did not allow the Constituent Assembly to meet beyond its first day. He sent the Red Guards to close it down and stop protests against its closure.
- The Bolsheviks had a majority in the **Congress of Soviets** and used this organisation to pass laws.
- Lenin wanted to create a **dictatorship** of the **proletariat** which would eventually lead to a truly communist system.

Political party	Seats won
Socialist Revolutionaries	370
Bolsheviks	175
Left-wing Socialist Revolutionaries	40
Mensheviks	17
Cadets	16
Others	89

The Bolsheviks' peace deal with Germany came at a great cost to Russia

- Lenin kept his promise to arrange peace. Trotsky led the negotiations and dragged the talks out hoping that a socialist revolution would occur in Germany. By February 1918 Germany lost patience and their troops advanced further into Russia.
- Lenin was forced to agree to peace and sign the Treaty of Brest-Litvosk in March 1918. Its terms were harsh but Lenin made sacrifices to save the revolution and may have suspected that Germany would eventually be defeated.
- Russia lost 34 per cent of its population; 32 per cent of its agricultural land; 54 per cent of industry; 26 per cent of railways; 89 per cent of coal mines and had to pay 300 million gold roubles to Germany.

Develop the detail

Each of the statements below is vague and lacks detail. On a separate piece of paper, add details to show that you understand the general point made. One example has been done for you.

Generalised statement	With developed detail
Lenin and Trotsky wanted to drag out the peace talks with Germany for as long as possible	The Bolsheviks expected there to be a socialist revolution in Germany so did not want to sign a peace deal that would be bad for Russia
Trotsky's attempt to delay peace talks with Germany did not work	
The Treaty of Brest-Litovsk was very harsh	
Lenin may have been wise to sign the harsh treaty	

 Support or challenge

In your exams you will often have to reach a judgement and support it with evidence. This task helps you practise. Read this statement:

'Lenin's decrees were more about increasing Bolshevik control than giving the Russian people their freedom.'

Below is evidence from this period. For each one, decide on whether it supports or challenges the overall statement above.

Decrees	Support	Challenge
Eight-hour working day introduced		
Cheka (secret police) established		
Land belonging to the Tsar and the Church given to the peasants		
Cadet Party banned		
Non-Bolshevik newspapers banned		
Workers given control of factories		

 Test yourself

1 List three decrees passed by the Bolsheviks in 1917.
2 What was the Constituent Assembly and why did Lenin close it after a day?

 Practice questions

1 Describe two problems faced by the Bolsheviks after the October Revolution. (4 marks)
2 In what ways were the lives of the Russian people affected by Lenin's decrees in March 1918? (8 marks)

TIP

Practise answering questions in timed conditions so you are prepared for the exam. Try to answer more than one question at a time as this is more realistic preparation. For the two practice questions on this page see if you can answer both in a total of fifteen minutes. You should write one detailed paragraph for every 4 marks, spending five minutes of writing time.

2.4 The causes and nature of the Civil War

The **Bolsheviks** used **force** to **maintain control** after the October Revolution

The Cheka (All-Russian Emergency Commission for Combating Counter-Revolution and Sabotage) and the Red Army provided the force to help Lenin stay in power. Lenin was even more willing to use violence after he survived an assassination attempt by a Socialist Revolutionary in August 1918.

> **Key point**
>
> The Bolsheviks had destroyed an attempt at democracy and signed the incredibly damaging Treaty of Brest-Litovsk. Although they had their supporters, the Bolsheviks had angered many different groups within Russia as well as their allies in the First World War. They had succeeded in uniting much of Russia against them.

Cheka	Red Army
• Created in December 1917 • A secret police like the Tsarist Okhrana • Agents were given the job of finding 'enemies of the state' such as army deserters, political opponents or people suspected of hoarding food • Members often ignored the Cheka code of conduct • It had 200,000 members by 1921 • It was brutal and greatly feared. It carried out the 'Red Terror' killing thousands of people • Later renamed the GPU, then NKVD and eventually KGB	• Small number of disciplined Red Guards led the takeover of Petrograd and Moscow in 1917 • A larger organisation was needed once the Bolsheviks were in power to deal with opposition • The Red Army was created in January 1918. All over-18s were eligible for service • Members were mostly peasants keen to protect the new government but there were some who came from the previous Tsarist army • Played a key role in the Russian Civil War which broke out in 1918

The **Bolsheviks** faced such a high level of **opposition** that there was a civil war

- The Civil War was fought between the Bolsheviks, or 'Reds', and a wide range of opposition groups known collectively as the 'Whites'.
- Very little united the Whites with the exception of their hatred of the Bolsheviks.
- Forces supporting the Whites included: Socialist Revolutionaries; Mensheviks; Cadets; Tsarist supporters; landlords and capitalists who had lost out due to the October Revolution.
- The Whites received support from outside Russia. Britain, France, Japan and the USA wanted Russia back in the war against Germany and wanted to prevent Russia from becoming communist.
- The Czech Legion, former prisoners of war, supported the Whites and took control of a section of the Trans-Siberian Railway.
- There were three White armies led by Generals Yudenich near Petrograd, Denikin near Moscow and Admiral Kolchak who marched on Moscow from central southern Russia.

The **fighting** during the **Civil War** was incredibly **brutal**

- Both sides committed atrocities and workers and peasants suffered the most in the areas where the fighting took place.
- Trotsky expanded the Red Army to over 300,000 men led by former Tsarist officers. Officers' families were taken hostage and political commissars watched them to ensure their loyalty.
- An intense period of violence known as the Red Terror followed:
  - The Cheka used beatings, hangings and shootings to prevent opposition within Bolshevik territories. Machine guns were turned on soldiers retreating against orders. Perhaps as many as 500,000 people were killed.
  - The Tsar and his family were murdered to prevent the Whites rescuing him and restoring him as leader.
  - The middle classes were oppressed and called up for compulsory labour.
  - Suspected political opponents were arrested and imprisoned without trial.
- White atrocities included burning down houses, whipping those suspected of supporting the Bolsheviks and forcing peasants to supply food and horses for their armies.

Spot the interpretation

Look at the interpretation below. Next to it are some inferences you can draw from it. Match these to specific parts of the interpretation.

INTERPRETATION A *Morgan Phillips Price*, My Three Revolutions, *1969. Price was a British journalist sent to report on the war in Russia. He initially supported the Bolsheviks but changed his mind and criticised the Party for taking too much power.*

The Red Terror now began. I shall never forget one of the *Isvestia* [a newspaper controlled by the Bolsheviks] articles for Saturday, September 7th. There was no mistaking its meaning. It was proposed to take hostages from the former officers of the Tsar's army, from the Cadets and from the families of the Moscow and Petrograd middle classes and to shoot ten for every communist who fell to the White terror. Shortly after a decree was issued by the Central Soviet Executive ordering all officers of the old army within territories of the Republic to report on a certain day at certain places. A panic resulted among the Moscow middle classes...

A   The Red Army was committing atrocities.

B   The White Army was committing atrocities.

C   Members of the former Tsarist army were being targeted by the Reds.

D   Members of the middle class were being targeted by the Reds.

E   The Reds were taking harsh revenge when any of their supporters were killed.

Practice questions

INTERPRETATION B *Albert Rhys Williams*, Through the Russian Revolution, *1921. Williams was an American socialist who met and admired Lenin. During the First World War he had taken photographs, including of German spies being executed by firing squad.*

My mind goes back to ... the tremendous obstacles it [the Soviet] confronted. And the odds seemed against it. In the first place the Soviet [controlled after October by the Bolsheviks] faced the same conditions that had overwhelmed the Tsar and Kerensky governments, i.e. the dislocation of industry, the paralysis of transport, the hunger and misery of the masses.

In the second place the Soviet had to cope with a hundred new obstacles – desertion of the intelligentsia [a group of highly educated and influential people], strike of the old officials, sabotage of the technicians, excommunication [to be refused the services and blessing of the Church] by the Church, the blockade by the Allies. It was cut off from the grain fields of the Ukraine, the oil fields of Baku, the coal mines of the Don, the cotton of Turkestan – fuel and food reserves were gone.

1   How does Interpretation A differ from Interpretation B about the behaviour of the Bolsheviks during the Russian Civil War?   [4 marks]

2   Why might the authors of Interpretation A and Interpretation B have different views about the behaviour of the Bolsheviks during the Russian Civil War?   [4 marks]

3   Which interpretation gives the more convincing opinion about the behaviour of the Bolsheviks during the Russian Civil War? Explain your answer based on your contextual knowledge and what it says in Interpretations A and B.   [8 marks]

Test yourself

1   What was the Cheka?

2   List three examples of groups who supported the Whites.

3   List two examples of Red atrocities and two examples of White atrocities during the Civil War.

TIP

All interpretations in the exam will have been written/published after the event being covered. However, you can still practise analysing influences on authors using extracts such as this one written during the Civil War rather than after.

2.5 The consequences of the Civil War and Bolshevik success

REVISED

Key point

Both the Whites and the Reds alienated large sections of society. The Civil War was not won because of Red popularity. The ruthless leadership of Lenin and Trotsky combined with Bolshevik control of the major cities and resources in Russia helped to bring about a Bolshevik victory.

The Bolsheviks won the Civil War in 1921 due to their organisation and discipline

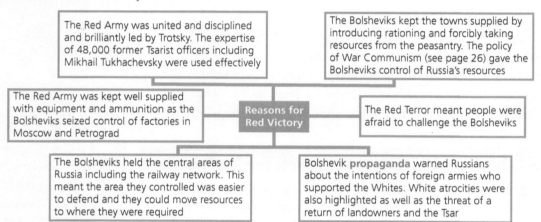

The Red Army was united and disciplined and brilliantly led by Trotsky. The expertise of 48,000 former Tsarist officers including Mikhail Tukhachevsky were used effectively

The Bolsheviks kept the towns supplied by introducing rationing and forcibly taking resources from the peasantry. The policy of War Communism (see page 26) gave the Bolsheviks control of Russia's resources

The Red Army was kept well supplied with equipment and ammunition as the Bolsheviks seized control of factories in Moscow and Petrograd

Reasons for Red Victory

The Red Terror meant people were afraid to challenge the Bolsheviks

The Bolsheviks held the central areas of Russia including the railway network. This meant the area they controlled was easier to defend and they could move resources to where they were required

Bolshevik propaganda warned Russians about the intentions of foreign armies who supported the Whites. White atrocities were also highlighted as well as the threat of a return of landowners and the Tsar

The Whites lost the Civil War due to their divisions and lack of support

- The Whites were neither as well-organised nor as united in their aims as the Reds.
- The White armies of Denikin, Yudenich and Kolchak were spread out around the edge of Russia. It was difficult to co-ordinate attacks. Trotsky was able to defeat the White armies one by one.
- Most Russians were peasants and they feared a return of landlords and therefore did not support the Whites.
- The involvement of foreign countries on the White side made them look unpatriotic.
- Both sides committed atrocities but Russian peasants were caused more suffering by the Whites. In Finland, the Whites executed almost 100,000 workers.
- 'Green' armies who supported the independence of their local area against interference and war took potential supporters from the Whites.

The Bolsheviks made effective use of propaganda to support their victory

- Both the Reds and the Whites used propaganda during the Civil War.
- Red propaganda was probably more effective due to the consistency of the messages. They focused on three things:
  1 The fight to protect workers' rights.
  2 The fight to remove foreign invaders.
  3 The fight against the re-establishment of aristocratic rule.
- Trotsky used the railway network to send out travelling cinemas showing propaganda films to local people and Red Army soldiers.
- Travelling cinemas were part of propaganda trains. The trains were painted with propaganda images and messages.
- Trotsky himself toured the country in his own war train. He made speeches, raised morale and delivered essential supplies.
- The Bolsheviks produced propaganda pamphlets. One pamphlet told the Russians that the 'working people had control of their country for the first time' and appealed to people to support the Reds.

Topic summary

Complete the pyramid below to summarise the key details of the topic.

- **One** White atrocity
- **Two** Bolshevik leaders
- **Three** messages of Red propaganda
- **Four** methods of Red propaganda
- **Five** of the Whites' weaknesses
- **Six** reasons for Red victory

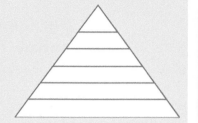

You're the examiner

Question 6 of your exam focuses on the most important cause of a particular event or consequence. For example:

Which of the following was the more important reason for Bolshevik victory in the Russian Civil War?

- **Propaganda**
- **Weaknesses of the Whites**

Explain your answer with reference to both reasons. **(12 marks)**

Below is one paragraph in answer to this question. Connect the comments to the highlighted elements to show the good features of the answer below.

> The weakness of the Whites was the most important reason for Bolshevik victory in the Civil War. The lack of unity and organisation was a significant weakness. Although the Whites had three armies they were led by three different people, Generals Denikin and Yudenich and Admiral Kolchak. This meant it was very difficult to co-ordinate attacks against the Reds. In addition to this, the three armies were positioned in different places around the country, Kolchak in the south, Yudenich near Petrograd and Denikin near Moscow. This resulted in further difficulties in trying to organise successful offensives against the Reds. The Whites' weaknesses were crucial in their defeat because they were unable to work together to attack

A Key words showing how the answer is organised.

B Relevant, detailed knowledge to support the argument.

C Key phrase to ensure you explain not just describe.

Test yourself

1 Why was Bolshevik control of the railway network so important to Red victory?

2 Why did foreign intervention on the side of the Whites actually help the Reds?

TIP

To help you ensure you have enough subject knowledge in every answer, try to include two detailed examples in every paragraph you write.

Practice question

Which of the following was the more important reason for Bolshevik victory in the Russian Civil War?

- Bolshevik control of the railway network
- Red Terror

Explain your answer with reference to both reasons. (12 marks)

2.6 War Communism and the Kronstadt Uprising

The policy of War Communism gave the Bolshevik government control of Russia's resources

- War communism was the economic policy introduced by the Bolsheviks during the Civil War.
- There were two main aims of War Communism:
  1 To begin to create communism in Russia by sharing resources more equally among the people.
  2 To win the Civil War by ensuring that workers in towns and the Red Army were supplied with food and weapons.

> **Key point**
>
> Lenin and the Bolsheviks were communists. They had a vision of a society in which people were equal and resources were shared fairly. However, they faced so much opposition and were so desperate to stay in control that they often introduced policies that were more about power than communism.

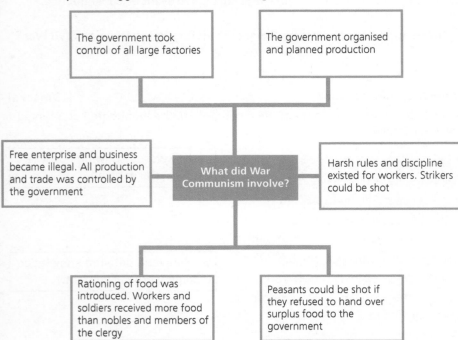

The government took control of all large factories

The government organised and planned production

Free enterprise and business became illegal. All production and trade was controlled by the government

What did War Communism involve?

Harsh rules and discipline existed for workers. Strikers could be shot

Rationing of food was introduced. Workers and soldiers received more food than nobles and members of the clergy

Peasants could be shot if they refused to hand over surplus food to the government

War Communism caused terrible hardship for the Russian people

- War Communism enabled the Bolsheviks to win the Civil War as they controlled Russia's resources, but this came at a terrible cost for Russian people.
- Some historians have argued that Lenin's attempt to quickly and ruthlessly create a communist society actually caused the Civil War.
- Peasants had no reason to produce more food. They could not make a profit and the government took any surplus goods away.
- The richest and most successful peasants (kulaks) were labelled 'enemies of the people' and had their land confiscated. There were not supposed to be rich people in a communist society but it was often the best farmers who had their land confiscated.
- Food shortages were caused by low production levels. Bad weather in 1920 and 1921 caused a famine. As many as 7 million people died in the famine. There were reports of cannibalism.
- Malnutrition encouraged the spread of disease, with a typhus epidemic causing the deaths of 3 million people in 1920.

The Kronstadt Uprising involved sailors violently opposing the Bolsheviks

- Kronstadt naval base was near Petrograd on an island in the Gulf of Finland. The Russian Baltic Fleet was stationed there.
- On 1 March 1921 the sailors at Kronstadt mutinied in response to unpopular Bolshevik policies.
- The mutiny was particularly terrible for Lenin as the Kronstadt sailors had been key supporters of the Bolsheviks during the October/November Revolution. It was also vital that the mutiny did not spread to other parts of the military.
- A list of fifteen demands was created by sailors on two of the leading battleships.
- Trotsky sent 60,000 troops to put down the uprising. More than 2,000 Kronstadt sailors were executed by the Cheka after the uprising.
- The mutiny shocked Lenin so much that shortly after the uprising he abandoned War Communism.

 Test yourself

1 What does communism mean?
2 List two aims of War Communism.
3 Why did Lenin take the Kronstadt Uprising so seriously?

 Topic summary

Complete the pyramid below to summarise the key details of the topic.
- **One** word to describe sailors overthrowing their commanders
- **Two** aims of War Communism
- **Three** consequences of the Kronstadt Uprising
- **Four** groups targeted for harsh treatment by War Communism
- **Five** examples of hardship caused by War Communism
- **Six** features of War Communism

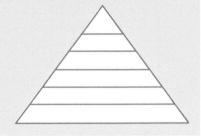

 Spot the mistakes

This paragraph attempts to answer the following question:
Describe two problems faced by the Bolsheviks during the Russian Civil War. **(4 marks)**
However, there are four factual mistakes in the paragraph. Find them and correct them.

> One problem faced by the Bolsheviks was how to create a capitalist society. The aim was to ensure that resources were distributed more unfairly than under the Tsarist system. The Bolsheviks introduced a system of rationing in which nobles and the clergy received more food than the workers and soldiers. Rich and successful peasants were labelled 'friends of the people' and had their goods confiscated. This was a problem because, in trying to create a more equal society, the Bolsheviks turned some of the Russian people against them.

 Practice question

In what ways were the lives of the Russian people affected by War Communism? **(8 marks)**

TIP

When answering any exam question make sure you use words such as 'because', 'therefore', 'this meant that' or 'so' to help you make a link between the information you include in your answer and exactly what the question is asking you to describe or explain.

2.7 The New Economic Policy (NEP) and the achievements of Lenin and Trotsky REVISED

Key point

Lenin's introduction of the NEP demonstrates that he was a pragmatic and flexible leader. By 1924 his bold decisions had left the Bolsheviks in power but with questions about how to create a communist society. Although the NEP helped the peasantry it was not as positive for the workers.

The New Economic Policy reintroduced capitalism for some parts of Russian society

- The New Economic Policy (NEP) was announced by Lenin at the Party Congress in March 1921.
- Lenin wanted to win the peasants' support. There had been peasant uprisings in the Tambov region in 1921 and the Bolsheviks used the Red Army to crush them. Force would not be enough in the long run.
- The NEP brought back capitalism to some parts of Russian society:
  - Peasants were allowed to make a profit by selling surplus grain.
  - **Grain requisitioning** – which meant peasants were forced to give the government some, or even most, of what they produced – was replaced by a **tax in kind**. This involved giving the government a much smaller amount of grain than previously, selling surplus grain and paying tax on what they sold.
  - Small factories in towns were put back into private ownership.
  - People were allowed to trade and make profit in small goods.
- The table shows how the NEP differed from War Communism:

Peasant production	War Communism	New Economic Policy
A peasant grows 10 tons of crops	Government takes 9 tons and leaves the peasant with 1 ton	Government takes 5 tons (50 per cent), the peasant sells 4 tons (pay tax on this) and is left with 1 ton plus cash
A peasant grows 1 ton of crops	Government takes none and leaves the peasant with 1 ton	Government takes half a ton (50 per cent) and the peasant is left with half a ton

The NEP did not apply to big business but many communists were shocked by the policy

- Lenin stated that the NEP was only a temporary measure to help Russia recover from the war and famine.
- Important **heavy industries** such as coal, iron, oil and steel would remain under the control of the government.
- Many Bolsheviks thought Lenin was betraying the Party's communist ideals.
- Lenin was able to persuade the Party to follow him.
- By 1925 the NEP had achieved some success. Food production had increased significantly. By 1926 the harvest had returned to 1913 levels.
- Between 1921 and 1925 the production of steel increased by five times, cattle numbers increased by 20 per cent and electricity output increased by four times.
- The pay of factory workers and miners remained below 1914 levels. Living conditions in cities remained overcrowded with families of seven living in one room.

By 1924 Lenin and Trotsky had overcome many challenges to ensure Bolshevik control of Russia

- Lenin successfully led the Bolsheviks through the October Revolution. He crushed the Constituent Assembly and ended Russia's involvement in the First World War.
- Lenin was helped by Trotsky. They successfully won the Civil War against the White armies and the intervention of foreign powers.
- Trotsky organised the Bolshevik Red Guards, which seized power in October/November 1917. He led the Red Army and played an important role in spreading propaganda during the Civil War.
- War Communism had been introduced to try to establish communism and to support the Bolsheviks' victory in the Civil War. Lenin was flexible enough to introduce the NEP in response to the Kronstadt mutiny and peasant uprisings.
- In 1922 the Russian empire was renamed the Union of Soviet Socialist Republics. The Bolshevik Party was renamed the Communist Party.
- Lenin suffered several strokes in 1922 and 1923. He died in January 1924.
- Historians disagree about whether Lenin or Trotsky were equally important to the Bolsheviks' success between 1917 and 1924.

Quick quizzes and answers at **www.hoddereducation.co.uk/myrevisionnotesdownloads**

Test yourself

1 List three successes of the NEP.
2 List three of Lenin's achievements.

 Spot the interpretation

1 Look at Interpretation A. Below it are inferences that could be drawn from it. Match each statement to a phrase or sentence that seems to support this inference.

> **INTERPRETATION A** *Victor Serge,* Memoirs of a Revolutionary, *1951.*
>
> The New Economic Policy was, in the space of a few months, already giving marvellous results. From one week to the next, the famine [was] diminishing. Restaurants were opening again and, wonder of wonders, pastries which were actually edible were on sale at a rouble [Russian currency] apiece. The public was beginning to recover its breath, and people were apt to talk about the return of capitalism ... On the other hand, the confusion among the Party rank-and-file [ordinary Party members] was staggering. For what did we fight, spill so much blood, agree to so many sacrifices? asked the Civil War veterans bitterly.

A The NEP was successful very quickly.
B There was evidence of private trade beginning again in the cities.
C People believed that capitalism was being reintroduced.
D Some members of the Bolshevik Party were upset with the introduction of the NEP.

2 For each inference, choose a piece of evidence that either supports or challenges the interpretation.

 Develop the detail

Each of the statements below is vague and lacks detail. On a separate piece of paper, add details to show that you understand the general point made. One example has been done for you.

Generalised statement	With developed detail
The NEP was a response to peasant unrest	There had been massive peasant uprisings in the Tambov region in 1921 and the Bolsheviks needed to win back the peasants' support
The NEP brought back capitalism to some parts of Russian society	
The NEP did not involve the government giving up control of all production	
The NEP was not as successful for workers in cities	

 Practice question

Which of the following was the more important reason that the Bolsheviks were able to maintain their control of Russia by 1924?

● Victory in the Civil War
● The introduction of the NEP

Explain your answer with reference to both reasons. (12 marks)

> **TIP**
>
> Use the first line of each paragraph in your answers to essay questions to make it clear what the paragraph is about and whether it is the most important cause in answer to the question.

3.1 The power struggle to succeed Lenin

REVISED

The top communists competed for power after Lenin's death

- Stalin: General Secretary. Ruthless political operator.
- Trotsky: Head of the Red Army and Civil War hero. Other Bolsheviks felt threatened by him. Wanted to replace the NEP with rapid industrialisation.
- Zinoviev and Kamenev: Local Party bosses of Leningrad and Moscow so only had local power bases.
- Bukharin: strong supporter of the NEP. Described by Lenin as 'the darling of the Party'. Editor of party newspaper *Pravda*.

> **Key point**
>
> Stalin sided with success which helped him win the power struggle. He worked with Bukharin while the NEP was working which undermined Trotsky. Stalin turned against Bukharin once Trotsky had been defeated and the NEP began to fail.

Stalin's position in the Communist Party helped him win the power struggle

Factor in power struggle	How it helped Stalin
Lenin's 'Last Testament'	This described and often criticised top Bolsheviks. Lenin suggested Stalin was rude and should lose his position as General Secretary. Stalin persuaded his rivals to keep the document secret and protected his position.
Luck	Trotsky became unwell at exactly the time Lenin was dying; he needed to be active in this period. The Head of the Cheka who disliked Stalin died in 1924.
Trotsky's challenge	Stalin tricked Trotsky into missing Lenin's funeral. Trotsky was arrogant and allowed Stalin to present himself as Lenin's closest ally.
Alliances	Stalin timed his alliances perfectly: the triumvirate with Kamenev and Zinoviev to weaken Trotsky; with Bukharin when the NEP was successful; turned on Bukharin when the NEP failed.
Position in the Party	As General Secretary, Stalin controlled Party membership and promotions. He was involved in deciding and implementing Party policy. Stalin's opponents underestimated him calling him the 'grey blur'. Trotsky did not use the Red Army to seize power, but Zinoviev and Kamenev feared he would, so initially worked against Trotsky. Bukharin did not use his position to help him win the power struggle.
Policies	Stalin's 'socialism in one country' was patriotic and popular. Trotsky's 'global revolution' seemed risky and involved sending Russian resources abroad.
Personality	Stalin was from a more ordinary background than his rivals; he seemed to be a man of the people, unlike the intellectual Trotsky.

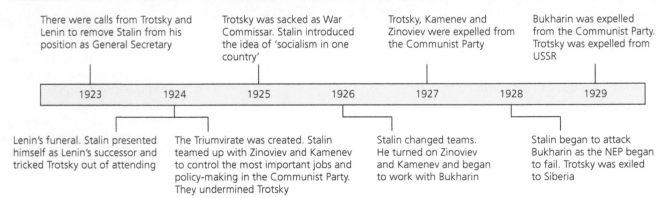

There were calls from Trotsky and Lenin to remove Stalin from his position as General Secretary

Trotsky was sacked as War Commissar. Stalin introduced the idea of 'socialism in one country'

Trotsky, Kamenev and Zinoviev were expelled from the Communist Party

Bukharin was expelled from the Communist Party. Trotsky was expelled from USSR

1923   1924   1925   1926   1927   1928   1929

Lenin's funeral. Stalin presented himself as Lenin's successor and tricked Trotsky out of attending

The Triumvirate was created. Stalin teamed up with Zinoviev and Kamenev to control the most important jobs and policy-making in the Communist Party. They undermined Trotsky

Stalin changed teams. He turned on Zinoviev and Kamenev and began to work with Bukharin

Stalin began to attack Bukharin as the NEP began to fail. Trotsky was exiled to Siberia

Timeline of Stalin's rise to power

Develop the explanation

Complete the table to explain why each of these reasons led to Stalin's victory in the power struggle.

Reasons	Explanations
Stalin's position in the Party as General Secretary	Stalin's position allowed him to control the membership of the Party as well as promotions. This meant that when the Party voted on policies and who to support Stalin had an advantage as he had filled the upper levels of the Party with his supporters
Trotsky's performance in the power struggle	
Luck	
Stalin's policy of 'socialism in one country'	

 Spot the mistakes

This paragraph attempts to answer the following question:

Describe two problems faced by Stalin during the power struggle. **(4 marks)**

However, there are three factual mistakes in the paragraph. Find them and correct them.

One problem faced by Stalin was Lenin's Last Statement. Lenin had criticised Stalin for being too polite and there was a risk that this could damage Stalin's reputation. Lenin had suggested that Stalin be removed from his position in the Party as First Administrator. This was a problem for Stalin as he needed to ensure that lots of people in the Communist Party did not see what Lenin had written.

 Test yourself

1 List the five main contenders to succeed Lenin as the leader of the Communist Party.
2 What was the Triumvirate and how did it help Stalin?

 Practice question

Which of the following was the more important reason why Stalin won the power struggle of the 1920s?

● Stalin's position in the Party
● The weaknesses of Stalin's opponents

Explain your answer with reference to both reasons. (12 marks)

TIP

When you have to remember lots of different factors related to one topic try to come up with a memory aid to help you. For example, you could use the 5Ps to help you remember why Stalin won the power struggle – position in the Party, policies, personality, performance, poor decisions of opponents.

3.2 Stalin the dictator: Communist control and the Terror

> **Key point**
>
> There is some debate about why Stalin organised the Terror. Suggestions range from his desire for political power, to paranoia about non-existent threats, to ensuring only loyal citizens remained should there be a war. Whatever the reason, by the end of the 1930s Stalin had created what some historians describe as a **totalitarian system** – a government in which one person is in total control.

The **Communist Party had total control** of the government and the country

- In 1936 the Stalin Constitution seemed to guarantee human rights and freedoms.
- Stalin actually used the **Politburo** to force his policies upon the country and control the population.
- There was only one legal political party in the country, the Communist Party. There was no alternative choice for the Soviet people in terms of who was running the country.
- The secret police (NKVD) helped Stalin to monitor and control the population, preventing any effective opposition.
- Strong armed forces with the latest equipment helped Stalin to intimidate and control the population.

Stalin organised **purges** of the Communist Party to **prevent** any challenges to his authority

- In 1934, Sergei Kirov was murdered. He was the popular leader of the Leningrad Communist Party.
- Stalin claimed Kirov's murder proved the existence of enemies who were trying to damage the USSR. Some historians have suggested Stalin organised Kirov's murder. Regardless, he used the murder as an excuse to 'purge' (remove) people who might challenge him in the Party.
- An estimated 500,000 Communist Party members were arrested and sent to labour camps (GULAGs) or executed. They were accused of anti-Soviet activities.
- Stalin even had the most important and loyal Bolsheviks who had been in the Party since before the October Revolution executed. Zinoviev and Kamenev were executed in 1936 and Bukharin in 1938. An NKVD agent went all the way to Mexico to murder Trotsky in 1940.

- Stalin tried to make the process look legal. 'Show trials' were organised in which forced confessions of treachery were given and then reported by the press.
- By 1940 almost every single person who had been involved in the 1917 October Revolution was dead apart from Stalin.

The **Great Terror** involved members of the **army** and **ordinary Soviet citizens** being targeted for punishment

- The NKVD and their new leader, Yezhov, took the lead in organising the Terror. Between 1936 and 1938 the arrests, exiles and executions spread to people outside the Communist Party. The worst year was 1937.
- The army was decimated with 25,000 officers removed from their positions. This even extended to the Supreme Commander of the Army, Mikhail Tukhachevsky.
- University lecturers, teachers, miners and engineers, factory managers and workers all disappeared. Everyone lived in fear. No one knew if they might receive the dreaded knock on the door in the middle of the night as this was when arrests took place.
- People were rarely told of the reason for their arrest. The official reasons were often spying for another country or deliberately wrecking the economy. These charges were almost never true but victims would be physically or psychologically tortured until they confessed to whatever they were accused of.
- By 1937 an estimated 18 million people had been transported to labour camps and 10 million had died.
- There remained 3 million people in GULAGs by 1939. Prisoners were forced to complete hard labour. GULAG prisoners helped the economy as they mined gold and built the Belomor Canal as well as roads and railways for no pay.
- Stalin ensured there were no challenges to his power or independent thinking as people were too afraid.
- The army was severely weakened. The lack of experienced and talented army officers threatened the USSR when Germany invaded in 1941.
- The whole country was weakened as so many talented individuals were removed from society.

Topic summary

Complete the following mind map to summarise the features of Communist Party control of the government.

This will make it easier to write analytical answers. Try to be as specific as possible as the mark schemes ask you to use specific, detailed knowledge. The first one has been started for you.

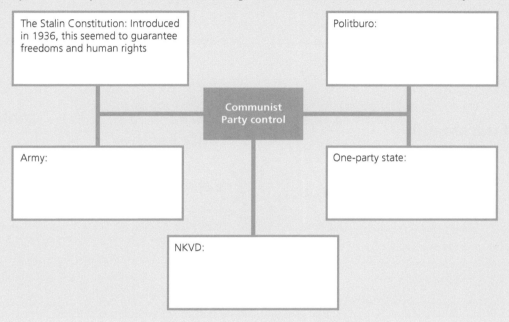

The Stalin Constitution: Introduced in 1936, this seemed to guarantee freedoms and human rights

Politburo:

Communist Party control

Army:

One-party state:

NKVD:

 ## Develop the detail

Each of the statements below is vague and lacks detail. Using the previous page and your own knowledge, on a separate piece of paper, add details to show that you understand the general point made. One example has been done for you.

Generalised statement on the impact of the Terror	With developed detail
The army was weakened	25,000 officers were removed from their positions including the Supreme Commander, Mikhail Tukhachevsky
The country as a whole was weakened	
Stalin had complete control of the country	
The population was afraid	

 ## Test yourself

1 What was the name of the head of Stalin's secret police who helped to carry out the Terror?

2 Who was Sergei Kirov and what did he have to do with the purges?

3 List two official reasons given for arrests during the Terror.

TIP

Think about the role of the Soviet people in carrying out the Terror as well as those who were victims or feared they might be. Some historians have suggested that the scale of the repression ran out of Stalin's control as people denounced one another to protect themselves – or even from a desire to take their manager's job, for example. Some communist officials were overly enthusiastic in finding 'enemies of the people' to impress Stalin.

 ## Practice question

In what ways were the lives of Soviet people affected by the Great Terror?   (8 marks)

3.3 Stalin's cult of personality

> **Key point**
>
> Stalin used a clever combination of new ideas and tradition as part of Soviet propaganda. Tsars had presented themselves as 'Little Fathers' to the Russian people and Stalin encouraged this idea of himself. Stalin also used the idea that Lenin was never wrong and suggested that he was following Lenin's path to make it harder for communists to challenge him.

A cult of personality was created to ensure Stalin's popularity

- Despite the Terror, Stalin was very popular in the 1930s. Soviet citizens believed that Stalin was a 'dictator of the people'.
- Statues and photographs of Stalin appeared everywhere. Every town had a Stalin square or Stalin avenue. Huge celebrations were organised to celebrate Stalin's birthday.
- When negative things happened Soviet citizens would blame Stalin's advisors and assume that Stalin himself was unaware that things were going badly.
- Propaganda was used very effectively to make Stalin appear as a hero, a father of his people and the true successor to Lenin.
- History was rewritten to exaggerate Stalin's role in the revolution. Photographs were changed to make Stalin appear more important or remove people who had fallen out of favour.
- Schoolchildren were expected to join the Young Pioneers where further indoctrination took place.

Propaganda and censorship covered every aspect of Soviet life

- Only communist-approved newspapers were allowed to publish. The most important were *Pravda* and *Izvestia*.
- Grand propaganda building projects such as the Moscow Metro were designed to show the success of the communist system. 70,000 libraries were built. Many towns gained sports and leisure facilities.

- Public events such as processions through towns praising the achievements of Stalin and the USSR were organised regularly.
- History lessons involved studying great Russian leaders such as Peter the Great. The suggestion was that Russia needed one powerful leader. Textbooks were changed as leaders were removed. Students would even have to tear out pages about Bukharin from books, for example.

Culture was also tightly controlled so only positive messages about Stalin and the Soviet Union were created

- A style of art called socialist realism became the only approved form of artistic expression. This gave clear positive messages about Stalin and life in the USSR. Art showed heroic workers, farmers and soldiers such as the painting *Collective Farm Workers Greeting a Tank*.
- The NKVD monitored all music and other arts.
- Poets, writers and playwrights praised Stalin. They could be arrested for being critical.
- An opera by composer Dmitri Shostakovich was criticised by Stalin in 1936. Shostakovich subtitled his next symphony 'A Soviet Artist's Practical Creative Reply to Just Criticism'.
- Most communists were not religious and the Russian Orthodox Church had been an important part of the Tsarist system. Religious services were banned. Monasteries were destroyed and only 1 in 40 churches held regular services. There were only 7 active bishops in the USSR. By 1939 there were only 1,300 mosques left out of the 26,000 in 1917.

 Test yourself

1. List two examples of propaganda aimed specifically at young people.
2. What was socialist realism?
3. List one example of art and one example of music that was produced in the 1930s.

Topic summary

Complete the following mind map to summarise the features of propaganda and censorship in 1930s Soviet Union.

This will make it easier to write analytical answers. Try to be as specific as possible as the mark schemes ask you to use specific, detailed knowledge. The first one has been started for you.

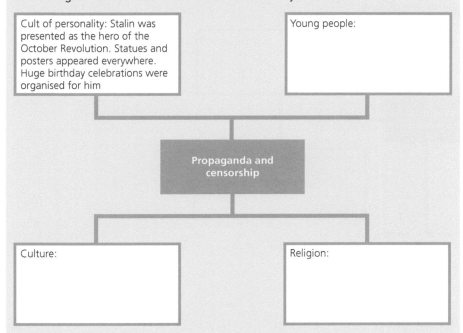

Cult of personality: Stalin was presented as the hero of the October Revolution. Statues and posters appeared everywhere. Huge birthday celebrations were organised for him

Young people:

Propaganda and censorship

Culture:

Religion:

 ## Develop the detail

Each of the statements below is vague and lacks detail. Using the previous page and your own knowledge, on a separate piece of paper, add details to show that you understand the general point made. One example has been done for you.

Generalised statement	With developed detail
Religious groups were persecuted in the Soviet Union	Monasteries were closed down and sometimes the buildings were blown up. The number of mosques decreased to just 1,300 by 1939
A cult of personality was created around Stalin	
Socialist realism was the approved form of culture	
Grand projects were used as part of propaganda	

TIP

Think about who is affected by the different types of propaganda. Everyone would be influenced by some aspects but only certain groups, such as children, would be directly impacted by the history lessons or Young Pioneers.

 ## Practice question

Describe two ways in which propaganda or censorship supported Stalin's popularity.

(4 marks)

3.4 Stalin's modernisation of the USSR: Collectivisation

Stalin wanted to modernise the USSR so it would become a successful communist country that could compete with other global powers

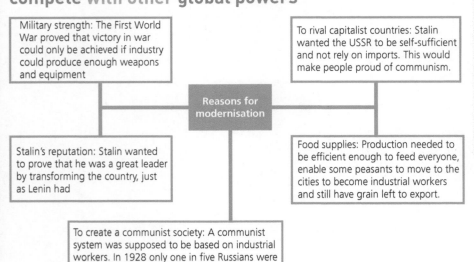

Military strength: The First World War proved that victory in war could only be achieved if industry could produce enough weapons and equipment

To rival capitalist countries: Stalin wanted the USSR to be self-sufficient and not rely on imports. This would make people proud of communism.

Reasons for modernisation

Stalin's reputation: Stalin wanted to prove that he was a great leader by transforming the country, just as Lenin had

Food supplies: Production needed to be efficient enough to feed everyone, enable some peasants to move to the cities to become industrial workers and still have grain left to export.

To create a communist society: A communist system was supposed to be based on industrial workers. In 1928 only one in five Russians were industrial workers; this needed to change

> **Key point**
>
> Collectivisation was a success for Stalin. It helped him win the power struggle by removing rivals who opposed it and gave him control of the resources to feed cities and support industrialisation. However, collectivisation came at a terrible human cost to the peasantry.

Collectivisation ended private ownership of land and gave the government control of the resources

- In 1928, the USSR needed two million more tons of grain to feed the cities. Stalin also wanted to export grain for profit to buy industrial goods.
- Under the NEP, most peasants had enough to eat and had no desire to change their farming methods to produce more for the cities.

Kulaks	Majority of peasants
• Owned small farms • Farms were too small for tractors, fertilisers and modern farming methods	• Worked as agricultural labourers • Did not own land

- **Collectivisation** meant peasants had to bring their land, tools and animals together to create new large farms called **kolkhoz**. Peasants were allowed to keep small plots for personal use.
- Machine Tractor Stations (MTS) organised agricultural equipment and seed for collective farms.
- Ninety per cent of kolkhoz produce would be sold to the state with the profits shared out. The peasants would feed themselves with the remaining ten per cent.

Collectivisation became a violent struggle and avoidable famine occurred

- Peasants were suspicious of government interference and the speed of change and did not want farms to be controlled by local communist leaders.
- Peasants did not want to grow new inedible crops such as flax. Government explanations and free seed did nothing to persuade them. There were 30,000 arson attacks protesting against collectivisation.
- Requisition parties were sent to forcibly take food from kulaks and other peasants who refused to hand over land and produce. Peasants were left to starve (see page 40).
- Collective farms were inefficient. Peasants were unfamiliar with new farming methods.
- Grain production initially decreased. The 1934 harvest was 6 million tons lower than the 1928 harvest. Peasants were angry as they starved while grain was exported to other countries. Five million tons of grain were exported in 1931, up from 0.03 million tons in 1928.
- Famines occurred in 1932–33 and millions died. Ukraine was the worst affected region.
- In 1935 the grain harvest was higher than the 1928 harvest. By 1941, 99 per cent of agricultural land had been collectivised.

Develop the explanation

Complete the table to explain why each of these reasons led to Stalin modernising the USSR.

Reasons	Explanations
Preparation for war	The First World War had revealed that only countries with successful industries that provided equipment and weapons could be victorious
Stalin's reputation	
Create a communist country	
Food supplies	

Spot the interpretation

Look at Interpretation A. Next to it are some inferences that you can draw from it.

Link each inference to specific details in the interpretation.

For each inference, add a specific piece of your own knowledge that supports or challenges this inference.

INTERPRETATION A *Isaac Deutscher, Stalin, 1949. Deutscher was a communist historian who supported Trotsky for criticising Stalin. He spent time in the Soviet Union during collectivisation.*

Within a short time rural Russia became pandemonium. The overwhelming majority of the peasantry confronted the government with desperate opposition. Collectivisation degenerated into a military operation, a cruel civil war. Rebellious villages were surrounded by machine-guns and forced to surrender.

Labels:

A Collectivisation was a chaotic process.

B Collectivisation was unpopular.

C Collectivisation involved the use of violence.

D The government was able to force the peasants to collectivise.

> **TIP**
>
> You can use a 'rule of three' to remember how to structure your answers to 8-mark interpretations questions:
> 1 What does the interpretation suggest?
> 2 What do you know about this topic?
> 3 Does your knowledge support or oppose the interpretation?

Test yourself

1 List three reasons why Stalin wanted to modernise.

2 What were kolkhoz?

Practice question

Which of the following was the more important reason for Stalin's introduction of collectivisation?

- Food supplies
- Creating a communist system

Explain your answer with reference to both reasons.   (12 marks)

3.5 Stalin's modernisation of the USSR: The Five-Year Plans

The **Five-Year Plans** used **time limits** and **targets** to force the **USSR** to **industrialise**

- GOSPLAN, created by Lenin in 1921, was in charge of planning for and organising industry.
- In 1921 GOSPLAN replaced the NEP with the Five-Year Plans. A quota system was introduced.
- Quotas (production targets and deadlines for hitting targets) were set by GOSPLAN for each industry, factory and worker. GOSPLAN's target for steel, oil and coal would be passed to regional officials, then factory managers, foremen and finally individual workers. Everyone had to play their part.

> **Key point**
>
> Historians have referred to the introduction of the Five-Year Plans and collectivisation as the 'Great Turn'. Lenin had taken a 'step back from socialism' by introducing the NEP in 1921. After winning the power struggle, Stalin forced the country to take a more direct route to communism under his leadership.

There were **three Five-Year Plans** between **1928** and **1941** and each had a **different set of priorities**

First Five-Year Plan, 1928–32	Second Five-Year Plan, 1933–37	Third Five-Year Plan, 1938–41
• Focused on heavy industry • Most targets were not met but huge increases in production achieved • Whole cities were built from nothing to gain access to resources in remote places such as Sverdlovsk in Siberia and Magnitogorsk in the Ural Mountains • Huge projects such as dams and hydro-electric power plants helped to meet industry's energy requirements	• Heavy industry remained the priority • New areas of focus also emerged such as mining for tin, lead and zinc • The chemical industry and electricity developed • Transport and communication was another new focus. Railways, canals and the spectacular Moscow underground railway were built	• Defence and armament production increased rapidly • Some factories were allowed to switch to the production of consumer goods • Heavy industry such as machinery and engineering continued to grow • The Plan was interrupted by the beginning of Russia's involvement in the Second World War in 1941

The **Five-Year Plans** rarely met their targets but there were **incredible increases in production**

- There was waste, inefficiency and even lying about production figures, but by 1941 the Soviet Union was an industrialised nation.

Industry	1927–28 production figure	1933 First Five-Year Plan *Target* vs. **Actual** production	1937 Second Five-Year Plan *Target* vs. **Actual** production
Coal (million tons)	35.4	*68* **64.3**	*1525* **1280**
Electricity (thousand million kilowatt hours)	5.05	*17* **13.4**	*38* **36.2**
Steel (million tons)	4	*8.3* **5.9**	*17* **17.7**

- Propaganda slogans such as 'achieve the Five-Year Plan in four years' encouraged people to fulfill their targets. Propaganda celebrated achievements praising Stalin and communism.
- Communist Party membership increased by 2 million during the first Five-Year Plan.

 Test yourself

1 What was GOSPLAN?
2 List three successes of the First Five-Year Plan.

Interpretations match

Below are four interpretations, four inferences and four examples.

1 Match the inferences to the interpretations.
2 Match the examples to the correct interpretation and inference.
3 Decide whether the example supports or opposes the interpretation.

Interpretation	Inference	Example
C. Ward, *Stalin's Russia* 'When the first Five-Year Plan was declared complete in December 1932 no major targets had been reached, but there were some dramatic advances'	The Plans were a success as demonstrated by new industries	Queueing outside food stores was a daily occurrence and there was a shortage of certain goods (see page 40)
A. Bullock, *Hitler and Stalin: Parallel Lives* 'After the grey compromises of the NEP, the Plan revived the flagging faith of the Party. Here at last was the chance to pour their enthusiasm into building the New Jerusalem they had been promised'	Production levels had increased significantly but not as much as had been planned	New cities such as Magnitogorsk were built as well as new hydro-electric plants and dams
M. Lewin, 'Society, state and ideology during the First Five-Year Plan' 'The falling standards of living, the lines outside stores … suggest the depths of the tensions and hardships'	Communist Party members supported the Five-Year Plans as they were about building a new society	The target for coal production was 1,525 million tons by the end of the second Five-Year Plan. Actual production was 1,280 million tons from a starting point of 35.4 million tons
S. Fitzpatrick, *On Stalin's Team* 'There really were achievements to celebrate … as far as heavy industry was concerned facts had sprung up on the ground all over the Soviet Union: new steel mills, tractor plants, blast furnaces…'	The Soviet people's quality of life suffered during the Plan	The 1934 Party Congress was themed the Congress of Victors to celebrate the achievements of industrialisation and 2 million new members joined the Communist Party during the First Five-Year Plan

 ## Practice question

Which interpretation is more convincing about the impact of the Five-Year Plans in the Soviet Union in the 1930s? (8 marks)

INTERPRETATION A *S. Davies,* Popular Opinion in Stalin's Russia: Terror, Propaganda and Dissent, 1934–41, *1997.*

Workers were acutely aware of fluctuations in their standard of living, frequently comparing prices with wages. It was patently obvious to them whether their own economic situation was improving or deteriorating, and they were not deceived by official rhetoric about rising standards.

INTERPRETATION B *Robert Service,* Stalin: A Biography, *2005.*

The GULAG, which was the network of labour camps subject to the People's Commissariat of Internal Affairs (NKVD), would be expanded and would become an indispensable sector of the Soviet economy … A great influx of people from the villages would take place as factories and mines sought to fill their labour forces. Literacy schemes would be given huge state funding…

TIP

In the exam the interpretations will be written within the dates of your course rather than by historians writing at a much later date. This means that you will have learnt something about the author themselves or the date of writing which will allow you to effectively answer Question 2 about why the authors of the interpretations may have different views. For 8-mark questions it is still worthwhile to practise using academic historians' work.

> **Key point**
>
> During the 1930s modernisation seemed to be more important than Communists' claims to be interested in equality. Stalin allowed a privileged elite to develop with incentives offered to encourage workers to hit production targets.

Collectivisation involved an attempt to destroy kulaks as a group in Soviet society

- Kulaks burned their own crops and killed their own animals rather than give them to the communists as part of collectivisation. The numbers of cattle, sheep and pigs fell by about 30 per cent between 1928 and 1934.
- Stalin announced that he wanted to 'liquidate the kulaks as a class'. This process was called dekulakisation.
- Thousands of kulak families were arrested and sent to GULAGs or exiled to areas where the land was not very fertile.

Industrial workers had to make the Five-Year Plans work and were bombarded with promises of rewards and punishments

- Stalin invited foreign specialists to the USSR to oversee industrial projects. Foreigners were impressed with the resilience of Russian workers.
- Discipline was harsh. Fines were imposed for workers who missed quotas, being late could result in sacking. Being sacked could involve losing your home.
- Many workers wanted to leave their jobs but were prevented from doing so as the NKVD introduced **internal passports**.
- Propaganda encouraged workers to become 'Stakhanovites' after Alexei Stakhanov, a 'Hero of the Soviet Union'. He had mined fourteen times his average quota of coal in one shift. Propaganda failed to show that he had received help.
- So called 'wreckers' and 'saboteurs' accused of damaging the economy were sent to labour camps for failing to hit their targets. Often they had not received proper training, made a mistake or been denounced by jealous colleagues.

Opportunities for women increased but they faced a dual burden

Soviet women in the 1930s

City dwellers' quality of life remained low but their security in relation to jobs and health improved

Positive aspects of life in cities in the 1930s	Continuing challenges
• Jobs could be well-paid with opportunities to earn bonuses for hitting targets. Unemployment was virtually non-existent • In 1940 there were more doctors per head of population than in Britain. Healthcare overall improved • Education was free and compulsory. Investments were made into college and workplace training schemes • Literacy was a high priority. Libraries were built • Many took pride in living in a successful communist regime • Sports facilities appeared in most towns	• Queueing was a part of everyday life with a scarcity of some items • Consumer goods such as radios and clothes were difficult to find • Housing was provided by the state but there was significant overcrowding. Often families slept, ate and lived in just two rooms • Wages fell between 1927 and 1938

Opportunities for an **emerging elite** provided luxuries **but undermined communist ideology**

- A wealthy elite was developing, contradicting communist theory about equality. The new class included foremen, managers, supervisors and technicians.
- Party members, Stakhanovites and officials in the growing state **bureaucracy** were rewarded with access to closed shops with luxury items and clothing, holidays and even private apartments.

 Test yourself

1 What did Stalin want to do to the kulaks?
2 List two terms for people accused of damaging the economy.

 Topic summary

Complete the pyramid below to summarise the key details of the topic.

- **One** 'Hero of the Soviet People'
- **Two** examples of kulak protest against collectivisation
- **Three** examples of new professionals
- **Four** examples of hardships for industrial workers
- **Five** facts about women's experiences of the 1930s
- **Six** positive aspects of city life in the 1930s

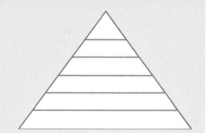

 Spot the interpretation

Look at Interpretation A. Next to it are some inferences that you can draw from it.

1 Link each inference to a specific quote in the interpretation.
2 For each inference, add a specific piece of your own knowledge that supports or challenges this inference.

INTERPRETATION A *Eugene Lyons*, Assignments in Utopia, *1937*.

The period of the Five-Year Plan has been christened Russia's 'Iron Age' ... I can think of no more apt description. Iron symbolises industrial construction and mechanisation. Iron symbolises no less the ruthlessness of the process, the bayonets, prison bars, rigid discipline and unstinting force, the unyielding and unfeeling determination of those who directed the period. Russia was transformed into a crucible in which men and metals were melted down and reshaped in a cruel heat, with small regard for the human.

Labels:

A The Five-Year Plans focused on industry.
B The Five-Year Plans involved harsh punishments.
C There were strict rules for workers.
D The communist leadership did not care about the impact upon people's lives.
E People suffered as a result of the Five-Year Plans.

 Practice questions

1 Describe two problems for city-dwellers in the USSR in the 1930s. **(4 marks)**
2 In what ways were the lives of women affected by the changes to Soviet society in the 1930s? **(8 marks)**

TIP

If you are worried about timing and completing all the questions in the exam, answer questions worth more marks first.

3.7 The impact of the Second World War

Stalin's wartime leadership began badly as he was surprised by the German invasion but Stalin became one of the key reasons for Soviet victory in the war

- Stalin had secured a ten-year non-aggression pact with Germany in 1939. He was worried about a Nazi invasion and Britain and France were not willing to enter into a protective agreement against Hitler.

- In 1941, Germany launched Operation Barbarossa: 2 million troops invaded the Soviet Union and 1,200 Russian aircraft were destroyed on the ground. Stalin had ignored warnings of the invasion.

- Reasons for Soviet victory included the following:

  ○ A 'scorched earth' policy was enacted as Russian forces retreated. This was a strategy that involved destroying resources that could be useful to the enemy.

  ○ The freezing Russian winters gave tens of thousands of German soldiers frostbite.

  ○ Hitler made tactical errors such as focusing on the city of Stalingrad and ignoring military experts.

  ○ The Cult of Personality meant people listened in awe to Stalin's speeches on the radio and he stayed in Moscow when it was under attack.

  ○ All of the Soviet Union's resources were focused on the war effort. Zhukov used 1.3 million soldiers to push the Germans out of the country.

As a dictator, Stalin's leadership was important in every aspect of the war

- Industrial production:

  ○ The Five-Year Plans meant Russia could produce the resources required to win the war. By 1944 industrial output had recovered to 1940 levels. The USSR produced twice as many machine guns and rifles as Germany.

  ○ The evacuation of Soviet industry saw 1,500 factories dismantled and rebuilt out of reach of the German armies.

- Propaganda:

  ○ The war was called the 'Great Patriotic War' and patriotic slogans such as 'Holy Mother Russia' instead of communist slogans were used to rally support.

  ○ The national anthem was changed so it was patriotic rather than a socialist anthem.

  ○ Propaganda showed the Nazis as evil and the atrocities they committed during the invasion backed this up.

- Military:

  ○ Stalin allowed military commanders such as Zhukov to use their expertise. Hitler did not do this.

  ○ Order 227, 'Not a step back', did not allow soldiers in the Soviet army to retreat. Machine gun regiments were placed behind soldiers to ensure they did not disobey.

> **Key point**
>
> Despite Stalin's ruthless treatment of the Soviet population, the cult of personality had worked and many people respected and even loved Stalin. It was not only this which made Soviet citizens fight so desperately in the war; Nazi atrocities and a sense of patriotism played their parts too.

The Soviet people made incredible sacrifices during the war which had a political, economic and social impact

Impact of the war	Examples
Social	• Over 25 million Soviet citizens (military and civilian) were killed. **Slavic peoples** were portrayed as sub-human in Nazi propaganda. This encouraged violence towards civilians as well as soldiers • More Soviet people died defending Stalingrad than the Americans lost in the entire war • Six million houses were badly damaged or destroyed • The working day was increased to twelve hours
Economic	• Huge areas of farmland including 100,000 collective farms were devastated • 2,000 towns and cities as well as 70,000 villages suffered major destruction • Around 60 per cent of Soviet coal and steel production and half the railway network was in German-occupied territory
Political	• Stalin and his government gave themselves even greater control of the population to ensure all resources and efforts were directed towards winning the war
Nationalities	• Stalin suspected some in the west of the Soviet Union, such as in the Ukraine, of pro-Nazi sympathies • Stalin had the NKVD transport whole national groups, such as the Tartars, to remote parts of the USSR. Thousands died on the journey or upon arrivall

 Spot the interpretation

Look at Interpretation A. Next to it are some inferences that you can draw from it.

1 Link each inference to specific details in the interpretation.

2 For each inference, add a specific piece of your own knowledge that supports or challenges this inference.

> **INTERPRETATION A** *Gregory Freeze*, Russia: A History, *2009*.
>
> One cannot disregard Stalin's positive contributions. First, for many Soviet citizens, he became a symbol of national unity, an embodiment of the spirit of resistance. Certain of his speeches and writings are said to have rallied the people and given invaluable boosts to their morale. Second, so great was the Terror that he inspired at the highest levels of Party and State that a rebuke from him, let alone a threat, could elicit impressive performances from factory managers and generals alike. Finally, although Stalin committed military blunders throughout the war, he improved as a strategist.

Labels:

A Stalin's contributions cannot be dismissed.

B Stalin helped to make the people feel united and positive.

C Stalinist repression scared people into achieving, or even exceeding, the goals set for them.

D Stalin got better as a military leader as the war progressed.

 Test yourself

1 List two facts about Operation Barbarossa.

2 What was the 'evacuation of Soviet industry'?

> **TIP**
>
> Whenever you are reading something you can practise your interpretations skills. Read the text, work out what it is suggesting about a topic – this is your inference. Then try to come up with a fact that either supports or opposes the inference you have made.

 Practice question

In what ways were the lives of the Soviet people affected by the Great Patriotic War? (8 marks)

Exam focus

Below are model answers for each of the question types. The annotations highlight what makes it a good answer.

INTERPRETATION A *Yurij Borisovich Yelagin, Memoirs, 1952. Yelagin was a violinist who left the Soviet Union for the USA because of the lack of freedom given to musicians. He wrote a book called* Taming of the Arts *to tell the rest of the world about cultural repression in the Soviet Union.*

At each town along the way, we saw hundreds and thousands of starving peasants at the station – with their last ounce of strength they had come from their villages in search of a piece of stale bread. They sat against the station walls in long dreary rows, sleeping, dying, and every morning the station guard would have the corpses removed on wagons covered with canvas.

INTERPRETATION B *Joseph Stalin, in conversation with Winston Churchill, August 1942.*

It was absolutely necessary for Russia, if we were to avoid periodic famines, to plough the land with tractors. When we gave tractors to the peasants they were all spoiled in a few months. Only collective farms with workshops could handle tractors. We took the greatest trouble to explain it to the peasants. It was no use arguing with them. After you have said all you can to a peasant he says he must go home and consult his wife. After he has talked it over he always answers that he does not want the collective farm and he would rather do without the tractors.

Question 1: How do interpretations differ?

How does Interpretation A differ from Interpretation B about collectivisation in the Soviet Union during the 1930s? Explain your answer based on what it says in Interpretations A and B. (4 marks)

Interpretation A suggests that collectivisation caused great hardship. It says, 'we saw hundreds and thousands of starving peasants' and 'the station guard would have the corpses removed'. The interpretation outlines the famine and deaths caused by the policy and the scale of the suffering. Interpretation B is different because it focuses on the reasons for the introduction of collectivisation and actually claims that it was necessary 'if we were to avoid periodic famines'. The interpretation also focuses on the role of tractors which would apparently stop the famines but then blames the peasants for resisting collectivisation and argues 'he would rather do without the tractors'. So Interpretation A focuses on the suffering of the peasants whereas Interpretation B focuses on the reasons for collectivisation and peasant resistance to it.

- Quotes are taken from the interpretations to show that they are different.
- The arguments of the interpretation are outlined.
- The answers finishes with a one-sentence summary of the differences between the interpretations.

Question 2: Why do interpretations differ?

Why might the authors of Interpretations A and B have different views on collectivisation in the Soviet Union during the 1930s? (4 marks)

Interpretation A was written by Yelagin who left the Soviet Union due to the repression in the 1930s. As he was writing in the USA he would have had the freedom to express his views. He was therefore able to tell the truth about the famine which resulted in the deaths of millions, with Ukraine the worst affected area. Yelagin would want to criticise collectivisation as he had been negatively affected by Stalin's policies himself.

Interpretation B came from Stalin himself. Stalin would want to blame the peasants for the famine rather than his own policy which he had continued with until 99 per cent of farms had been collectivised by 1941. The date of the interpretation is important because the conversation was during the Second World War. This meant that Stalin was talking to one of his wartime allies who he would want to reassure and claim that he was a leader who made good decisions, could be trusted and was worth fighting alongside.

- Information about the provenance is used to explain the motive of the author.
- Own knowledge is used to support the comments about the provenance.
- Developed explanation about the motive of the author.

Question 3: How convincing are these interpretations?

Which interpretation gives the more convincing opinion about collectivisation in the Soviet Union during the 1930s? Explain your answer based on your contextual knowledge and what it says in Interpretations A and B. (8 marks)

Interpretation A is very convincing in describing the suffering that collectivisation caused. It mentions the hundreds of thousands of starving peasants seen in one location. This is accurate because, in total, millions of peasants across the Soviet Union died between 1932 and 1933. The extract mentions that the dead had to be taken away on wagons and this reflects the situation in Ukraine where most victims of the famine lived.

Interpretation B is convincing in relation to the issue of peasant opposition. Stalin states that peasants 'did not want the collective farm' which can be supported by the fact that there were 30,000 arson attacks in protest against the policy. However, Interpretation B suggests that collectivisation was necessary to prevent famines. This is not convincing because the policy involved continuing to export 5 million tons of grain in 1931 which helped to cause famine.

Therefore, although aspects of both interpretations are convincing, Interpretation A is more convincing because it is accurate in the one aspect it focuses on. Interpretation B, on the other hand, makes suggestions which can be disproven.

- The answer identifies claims made by the interpretations.
- Own knowledge is used to support or oppose the interpretation.
- The answer links back to the question and uses the word 'convincing'.
- An overall judgement is reached, showing briefly why one interpretation is more convincing.

Question 4: Describe two...

Describe two problems faced by the Tsar during the First World War.
(4 marks)

One problem faced by the Tsar was the military defeats. At the Battle of Tannenburg and the Battle of the Masurian Lakes the Russian army was badly defeated. This was a problem because it affected the morale of the Russian army and people and ultimately losing battles meant losing the war.

Another problem was the impact the war had on the people in the cities. In 1917 a worker's wages would buy one-third of a bag of flour in comparison with two bags in 1914. This was a problem as the workers were hungry and therefore less productive and more angry with the Tsar.

- Two points which are relevant to the question have been identified.
- Own knowledge has been included to support the point being made.
- The answer directly addresses the question. The word 'problem' from the question has been used to focus the answer.

Question 5: In what ways...?

In what ways were the lives of the Russian people affected by the Russian Civil War? (8 marks)

One change caused by the Russian Civil War was the incredibly brutal violence which much of the population experienced. Both the Reds and the Whites carried out atrocities. The Whites burned down houses and whipped Bolshevik supporters while the Reds used beatings, shootings and hangings. This was an important change because of the scale of the violence. During the Tsarist period hundreds of people, often poorer members of society, were injured and killed during protests. During the Civil War thousands of people from all sections of society were being tortured and executed.

A second change caused by the Civil War was the impact of Bolshevik propaganda upon the attitudes of the population. Trotsky had his own propaganda train to spread the idea that the Bolsheviks were on the side of the workers and that the Whites would reintroduce aristocratic rule. This had a very powerful impact on Russian workers and peasants. Even if they did not wholly support the Bolsheviks, propaganda helped to encourage them to support changing Russian society. Everyone experienced the violence during the conflict but it was mostly only the poorest in society who had their attitudes changed. They were persuaded by the Bolshevik propaganda and the idea that their lives could improve, this was not the case for the landowners and politicians on the White side.

- Each paragraph opens with one clear point that addresses the question.
- Specific, detailed subject knowledge has been included.
- Links are made back to the question using developed explanations about change.
- The answer explains how the changes did not have the same effect on everyone.

Question 6: Which reason?

Which of the following was the more important reason for the collapse of Tsarism in 1917?

- **The role of opposition**
- **The mistakes of Nicholas II**

Explain your answer with reference to both reasons. (12 marks)

The Tsar's own mistakes were the most important reason for the collapse of Tsarism. Nicholas believed firmly that God had made him Tsar and was reluctant to bring about changes to give the Russian people more of a say in ruling Russia. Even when the Duma was introduced after 1905, Nicholas had Stolypin change the electoral laws so many people did not really have a voice and the Duma would not bring about change. This made Tsarism more likely to collapse as people realised that this system was not helping them lead successful lives. During the First World War, Nicholas made the mistake of becoming commander-in-chief of the army which meant that every military defeat was blamed directly on him. It also involved leaving the Tsarina and the unpopular Rasputin to rule in St Petersburg. This made government more chaotic, less effective and increased the anger people felt towards Tsarism.

The role of opposition contributed to the collapse of Tsarism. In 1905 at Bloody Sunday, peaceful protesters were shot at by Tsarist forces for simply asking for improvements to their living and working conditions. The marchers had shown that the Tsar was failing to provide for the Russian population. During the First World War the Council of United Nobility demanded that the Tsar abdicate and the Petrograd Soviet was established in 1905 and again in 1917. Opposition groups were proving that there were alternatives to Tsarist rule available. The fact that the opposition groups included all sections of society, from workers in the Soviet to landowners in the Council of United Nobility, also proved how unpopular the Tsar was. It was impossible for Nicholas to rule with most people in the country against him.

In conclusion, Nicholas II was ultimately responsible for the fall of Tsarism. His mistakes weakened the country and contributed significantly to Russia's defeat in the war which helped turn the population against him. His mistakes are linked to the role of opposition as Nicholas' actions encouraged opposition groups to form and his responses to their actions always seemed to make people even more determined to bring about revolution.

- Each paragraph addresses one of the reasons given in the question.
- The answer includes relevant, detailed own knowledge.
- The answer links back to the question and explains the importance of each reason.
- The answer gives a judgement about which reason is more important and uses a link between the two reasons in the question to support this judgement.

Glossary

Abdicate   To give up the throne

Aristocracy   The upper class in society; often people in this group had hereditary titles

Autocracy   A system of government in which power is held by one person

Bolshevik Party   A political party led by Lenin which aimed to organise a revolution and implement communist policies

Capitalist   A follower of capitalism, meaning a system in which privately owned businesses have the freedom to trade, invest and make profit as opposed to government controlling the economy

Collectivisation   The process in the Soviet Union between 1929 and 1940 in which private ownership of farms was abolished and peasants' land and resources were brought together in large, shared farms known as collective farms

Communist   A follower of communism, a system in which the government controls and shares resources in order to create and maintain an equal society

Congress of Soviets   Local soviets from around the country sent delegates to meet, discuss policy and elect a Supreme Soviet to represent the whole country

Constituent Assembly   An elected group of representatives who are brought together to draw up a new constitution

Council of Ministers   Created in 1906 to make policy, the Council brought together the leaders of the different government departments and was led by a Chairman who was effectively the Prime Minister

Council of the United Nobility   An organisation of the aristocracy created to defend the rights of the landowning classes. It strongly supported autocracy

Decree   An official order that has the force of law

Democracy   A system of government in which citizens have the right to vote in elections and choose their representatives

Dictatorship   A system of government in which one person has absolute control

Duma   The elected assembly created in 1906 with the power to discuss policies and laws, though it could not enact new laws itself. The Tsar had the power to dismiss the Duma

Grain requisitioning   A policy which involved taking grain and other agricultural products from peasants either in exchange for a fixed price or by force

GULAGs   A system of labour camps in which prisoners were forced to work

Internal passports   A system which prevented free movement of workers within the USSR.

Kolkhoz   A collective farm run on state-owned land by groups of peasant households

Liberal   A view which supports the idea of individuals having the freedom to make their own choices about their life and beliefs

Mir   A peasant community in Tsarist Russia which elected elders and governed itself in relation to local issues

Octobrist Party   The Union of 17 October was a political party created to support the promises made in the October Manifesto. Until 1915, Octobrists were strongly in favour of Tsarist government. Made up of members of the nobility, Octobrists wanted to retain their own privileged position in society

Okhrana   The Tsarist secret police

Politburo   The most important decision-making body in the Communist Party

Progressive Bloc   An alliance of political parties in the Duma who aimed to pressure the Tsar to accept reforms during the First World War

Proletariat   The working classes

Propaganda   Information aimed to persuade people of a certain viewpoint

Radical   The idea of supporting a significant or complete change

Red Guard   Volunteer paramilitary groups who aimed to protect soviet power

Reformist   Someone who wants to bring about gradual change

Slavic peoples   Many people in Russia are Slavic, meaning they share some cultural and religious ideas. The Nazis attacked this group in their propaganda.

Socialist realism   The government-approved form of art from 1932. Artists, musicians, writers and all cultural figures were to produce work with positive, easy-to-understand messages about life in the Soviet Union

Socialist Revolutionaries   A political party which aimed to overthrown the Tsar and provide peasants with shared land ownership

Soviet   Elected councils often made up of workers or soldiers

Sovnarkom   The Council of People's Commissars. The organisation which acted as a cabinet in the Soviet Union. It brought together the heads of the different government departments and was chaired by a President

State Council   An upper chamber created in 1906 to cancel out the powers of the Duma. Half the representatives were elected by the nobility and half were appointed by the Tsar

Tax in kind   Taxes paid in goods or services rather than money

Totalitarian system   A system of government in which one person has total control

Triumvirate   A group of three people who work together

Trudovik   A political party which broke away from the Socialist Revolutionaries. They disagreed about whether to participate in the first Duma. The Trudoviks did and the Socialist Revolutionaries did not

Winter Palace   The official residence of Russian Tsars

Zemgor   Brought together the Union of Zemstvos and the Union of Towns to help the government during the First World War

Zemstva   Local government under the Tsarist system, dominated by the nobility

Zhukov   A military general who played a crucial part in the Great Patriotic War. He organised the defence of cities such as Moscow and Stalingrad.